THE GLENBROOKE SERIES

Titles in the Glenbrooke Series

Secrets

ROBIN JONES GUNN

Multnomah®Publishers *Sisters, Oregon*

SECRETS
published by Multnomah Publishers, Inc.
© 1995 by Robin's Ink, LLC
International Standard Book Number: 1-59052-673-2

Cover design and images by Steve Gardner/His Image PixelWorks

Multnomah is a trademark of Multnomah Publishers, Inc., and is
registered in the U.S. Patent and Trademark Office.
The colophon is a trademark of Multnomah Publishers, Inc.

Printed in the United States of America

For information:
MULTNOMAH PUBLISHERS, INC.
POST OFFICE BOX 1720
SISTERS, OREGON 97759

Library of Congress Cataloging-in-Publication Data:

Gunn, Robin Jones, 1955–
Secrets/by Robin Jones Gunn.
   p.cm.
   ISBN 0-88070-721-6
       1-57673-420-X
       1-59052-240-0
       1-59052-673-2
   I. Title.
PS3557.U4866S43 1994
813'.54—dc20   94–43679
                                          CIP
       05 06 07 08 09 —18 17 16 15 14 13

For Marlee Alex
a gentle woman of compassion
a gifted crafter of words
my dearly esteemed friend

And for my neighbors on Butterfly Court.
I love you guys!

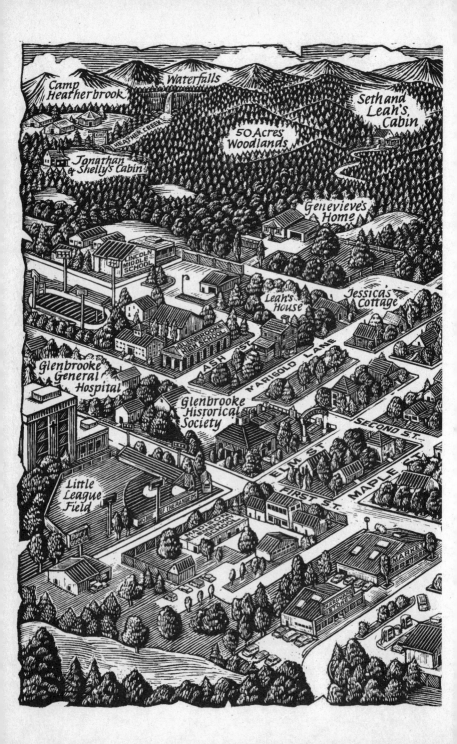

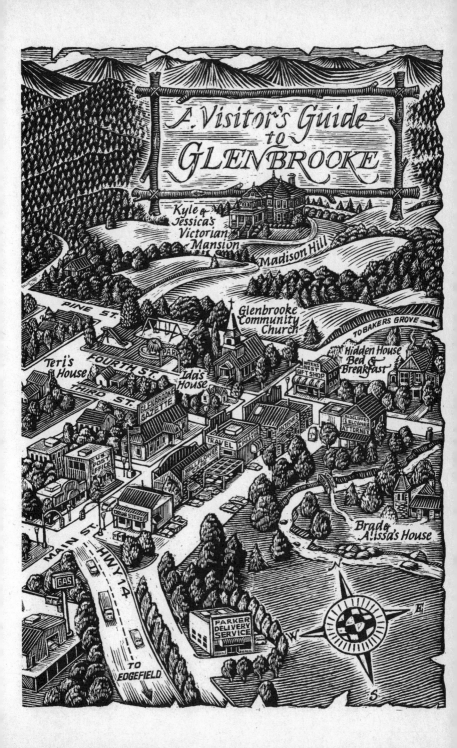

Would not God search this out?
For He knows the secrets of the heart.

PSALM 44:21, *NEW KING JAMES* VERSION

Chapter One

essica Morgan gripped her car's steering wheel and read the road sign aloud as she cruised past it. "Glenbrooke, three miles."

The summer breeze whipped through her open window and danced with the ends of her shoulder-length, honey-blond hair.

"This is it," Jessica murmured as the Oregon road brought her to the brink of her new life. For months she had planned this step into independence. Then yesterday, on the eve of her twenty-fifth birthday, she had hit the road with the back seat of her used station wagon full of boxes and her heart full of dreams.

She had driven ten hours yesterday before stopping at a hotel in Redding, California. After buying Chinese food, she ate it while sitting cross-legged on the bed watching the end of an old black-and-white movie. Jessica fell asleep dreaming of new beginnings and rose at 6:30, ready to drive another nine hours on her birthday.

I'm almost there, she thought. *I'm really doing this! Look at all these trees. This is beautiful. I'm going to love it here!*

The country road meandered through a grove of quivering willows. As she passed them, the trees appeared to wave at her, welcoming her to their corner of the world. The late afternoon sun shot between the trees like a strobe light, striking the side of her car at rapid intervals and creating stripes. Light appeared, then shadow, light, then shadow.

As Jessica drove out of the grouping of trees, the road twisted to the right. She veered the car to round the curve. Suddenly the bright sunlight struck her eyes, momentarily blinding her. Swerving to the right to avoid a truck, she felt her front tire catch the gravel on the side of the road. Before she realized what was happening, she had lost control of the car. In one terrifying instant, Jessica felt the car skid through the gravel and tilt over on its side. Her seat belt held her fast as Jessica screamed and clutched the steering wheel. The car tumbled over an embankment, then came to a jolting halt in a ditch about twenty feet below the road. The world seemed to stop.

Jessica tried to cry out, but no sound came from her lips. Stunned, she lay motionless on her side. She quickly blinked as if to dismiss a bizarre daydream that she could snap out of. Her hair covered half her face. She felt a hot, moist trickle coursing down her chin and an acidic taste filling her mouth. *I'm bleeding!*

Peering through her disheveled hair, Jessica tried to focus her eyes. When her vision began to clear, she could make out the image of the windshield, now shattered, and the mangled steering wheel bent down and pinning her left leg in place.

Suddenly her breath came back, and with her breath came the pain. Every part of her body ached, and a ring of white dots began to spin wildly before her eyes, whether she opened or closed them. Jessica was afraid to move, afraid to try any part of her body and find it unwilling to cooperate.

This didn't happen! It couldn't have. It was too fast. Wake up, Jess!

Through all the cotton that seemed to fill her head, Jessica heard a remote crackle of a walkie talkie and a male voice in the distance saying, "I've located the car. I'm checking now for survivors. Over."

I'm here! Down here! Help! Jessica called out in her head. The only sound that escaped her lips was a raspy, "Ahhgg!" That's when she realized her tongue was bleeding and her upper lip was beginning to swell.

"Hello in there," a male voice said calmly. The man leaned in through the open driver's window, which was now above Jessica on her left side. "Can you hear me?"

"Yeath," Jessica managed to say, her tongue swelling and her jaw beginning to quiver. She felt cold and shivered uncontrollably.

"Don't try to move," the deep voice said. "I've called for help. We'll get you out of there. It's going to take a few minutes, now, so don't move, okay?"

Jessica couldn't see the man's face, but his voice soothed her. She heard scraping metal above her, and then a large, steady hand touched her neck and felt for her pulse.

"You had your seat belt on. Good girl," he said. The walkie talkie crackled again, this time right above her.

"Yeah, Mary," the man said. "We have one female, mid-twenties, I'd say. Condition is stable. I'll wait for the ambulance before I move her. Over."

Jessica felt his hand once more, this time across her cheek as he brushed back her hair. "How ya' doin'? I'm Kyle. What's your name?"

"Jethica," she said, her tongue now throbbing. From the corner of her eye she caught a glimpse of dark hair and a tanned face.

"I saw your car just as it began to roll. Must have been pretty scary for you."

Jessica responded with a nod and realized she could move her neck painlessly. She slowly turned her head and looked up into her rescuer's face. Jessica smiled with surprise and pleasure when she saw his green eyes, straight nose, windblown dark hair, and the hint of a five o'clock shadow across his no-nonsense jaw. With her smile came a stabbing throb in her top lip and the sensation of blood trickling down her chin.

"So, you can move a little, huh?" Kyle said. "Let's try your left arm. Good! That's great. How do your legs feel?"

Jessica tried to answer that the right one felt okay, but the left one was immobile. Her words came out slurred. She wasn't sure exactly what she said. Her jaw was really quivering now, and she felt helpless.

"Just relax," Kyle said. "As soon as the guys arrive with the ambulance, we'll get you all patched up. I'm going to put some pressure on your lip now. Try breathing slowly and evenly like this." Kyle leaned toward her. His face was about six inches from hers. He began to breathe in slowly through his nose and exhale slowly through his mouth. The distinct smell of cinnamon chewing gum was on his breath, which she found strangely comforting.

Jessica heard the distant wail of an approaching siren. Within minutes she was in the middle of a flurry of activity. Some of the men began to stabilize the car while several others cut off the door to have more room to reach her. Soon a team of steady hands undid Jessica's seat belt, removed the steering wheel, and eased her body onto a long board. They taped her forehead to the board so she couldn't move her head, and one of the men wrapped her in a blanket. They lifted the stretcher and with sure-footed steps walked up the embankment and carried her to the ambulance.

Jessica felt as if her eyelids weighed a hundred pounds. They clamped shut as her throbbing head filled with questions.

Why? Why me? Why now, right on the edge of my new beginning?

With a jolt, the men released the wheeled legs on the stretcher and slid Jessica into the back of the ambulance. One of them reached for her arm from underneath the blanket, and running a rough thumb over the back of her left hand, he asked her to make a fist.

Another paramedic spoke calmly, a few inches from her head, "Can you open your eyes for me? That's good. Now can you tell me where it hurts the most?"

"My leg," Jessica said.

"It's her left one." Jessica recognized Kyle's strong voice. His hand reached over and pressed against her upper lip once more.

The siren started up, and the ambulance lurched out onto the road and sped toward the Glenbrooke hospital.

As the stretcher jostled in the ambulance, the paramedic holding Jessica's left hand said, "Keep your fist. This is going to pinch a little bit." And with that an IV needle poked through the bulging vein on the top of her hand.

"Ouch," she said weakly.

She felt a soft cloth on her chin and lips and opened her eyes all the way. Kyle smiled at her. With one hand he pressed against her lip, and with the other he wiped the drying blood from her cheek and chin.

"Can you open your mouth a little? I need to put this against your tongue," he said, placing a swab of cotton between her tongue and cheek. "The bleeding looks like it's about to stop in there. Now if we can only get your lip to cooperate, you'll be in good shape. We'll be at the hospital in a few minutes. You doing okay?"

Jessica tried to nod her head, but the tape across her forehead held her firmly in place. She forced a crooked, puffy-cheeked smile beneath the pressure of his hand on her lip.

Jessica felt ridiculous, trying to flirt in her condition. Here was the most handsome, gentle man she had ever laid eyes on, and she was a helpless mess.

He's probably married and has six kids. These guys are trained to be nice to accident victims.

The full impact of her situation hit Jessica. She *was* a victim. None of this was supposed to happen. She was supposed to enter Glenbrooke quietly and begin her new life uneventfully. Yes, even secretly. Now how would she answer the prying questions she was sure to receive at the hospital?

At least she had Mr. McGregor, her old English teacher from high school. He was the only soul she knew in Glenbrooke, and when he had answered her letter two months ago, he had promised her a job teaching at Glenbrooke High and had even offered to find a place for her to live.

"Here we are," Kyle said as the ambulance bumped into the hospital parking lot.

Jessica closed her eyes again. The stretcher was manhandled out of the ambulance, into the emergency room, and behind a curtained area where her IV sack was hung. A white-coated doctor immediately appeared.

The pain surged over Jessica's body again, and she shivered under the bright lights as the doctor and paramedics discussed her condition in their abbreviated lingo. She could tell that Kyle was still by her side because of the constant pressure he was placing on her lip. "Can someone grab a couple of warm blankets?" he asked.

A few moments later Jessica felt a heated blanket being

placed over her. She thought the sensation was the most wonderful in the world.

Forcing her eyes open a slit, she saw another face loom
over her. This one was a red-haired nurse wearing blue-
rimmed glasses and bright orange lipstick.

"I have just a few questions for you, dear," she said, adjusting the paper on her clipboard and reading the list before her.
"What is the name of your insurance carrier? And do you have
your card with you?"

"I, I don't have one," Jessica mumbled, her lip now swollen
twice its normal size.

"You don't have your card? Then do you know the name of
your insurance company?"

"No."

"What *kind* of insurance do you have, dear?"

"I don't…"

"You don't have insurance?"

"No."

"I see. Well, then, are you married?"

"No."

"I need the name of a relative, dear."

Jessica hesitated before finally answering, "None."

"You have *no* relatives?" The woman sounded irritated. "No
insurance and no relatives?"

Jessica didn't answer.

"Perhaps we should begin with a few simpler questions.
What is your full name?"

"Jessica…." She halted. Giving her last name could ruin
everything. Quickly she forced her eyes open and searched for
a clue as to what to say. All she could see, with her head still
strapped to the board, was a box of surgical supplies on a shelf
in the corner of the room. The bold letters spelled out "Fenton
Laboratories."

"Fenton," she said through stiff, swollen lips.

"Jessica Fenton," the woman repeated as she filled out her form. "And your address?"

"I don't know…"

"Do you know your phone number or the number of someone we can call?" The voice was patronizing.

Jessica paused. "No."

"Honey, before we can begin treatment, we need some cooperation here. The hospital requires a deposit today of one hundred dollars. Will you be able to pay that, or do you need financial assistance?"

"I'll pay." Jessica was beginning to feel woozy, and the questions from this orange-lipped woman weren't helping any. She forced herself to say, "My purse."

"It must be at the accident site," Kyle said. "Look, Betty, can't you work this out later? She's obviously been through a lot, and once she retrieves her purse she can give you all the information you need. Can't you see she's not up to answering your questions right now?"

"It's hospital policy, Kyle. You know that!"

Kyle left the cotton on Jessica's lip and stepped away from her bed, pulling Betty along with him. Jessica could hear him speak in hushed tones from somewhere in the corner, giving Betty his opinion of hospital policy.

The doctor stepped back over to Jessica's side and began his examination by removing the bloodied cotton and checking her tongue and lip. "Looks okay inside there. We will need a few stitches on this upper lip," he said.

Jessica shut her eyes as the team of medical personnel went to work, first with an injection to numb her lip and then with eight—or was it ten?—precise stitches. She could feel the tight tugs as her lip was sewn up, but that was about the only part of her body that felt no pain, thanks to the local anesthetic.

Another doctor continued the exam while the stitches were put in place. "Does this hurt?" he asked, proceeding to press her jaw, check her ears, and probe her rigid body, poking and jabbing at every tender spot. Everything hurt. Everything except her weird lip, which felt ten times its normal size and useless.

When the doctor reached her left leg, he stopped and ordered she be taken in for X rays as soon as the stitches were completed. As they wheeled her down the hall, Jessica listened for Kyle's voice and tried her best to see him in the blur of medical assistants, but he was gone.

For the next few hours Jessica underwent a variety of tests, X-rays, and pokings. Some kind of pain reliever or sedative had been injected into her IV earlier, and she began to experience the effects of it. She felt sleepy, and everything around her looked fuzzy. At one point, she opened her eyes and noticed a large wall clock with thick, black numbers. It read 6:35.

The next time she opened her eyes and tried to focus on her surroundings, the room was much darker. Jessica realized she was lying in a hospital bed, although she didn't remember being placed there. Everything felt mushy and out of focus.

She fell back asleep until a nurse came in to check on her sometime later. Jessica tried to stretch as the nurse checked her pulse and found that she could focus and think more clearly. She could also feel the pain since the buffer of medication was wearing off.

"How are you feeling?" the young nurse asked.

"I hurt," Jessica answered, her tongue and lip still feeling puffy and painful.

"The doctor will check on you in a few minutes."

He appeared on cue, wearing a white coat, thick-rimmed glasses, and a stethoscope around his neck. "I'm Dr. Laughlin. I have good news for you, Miss Fenton."

Miss Fenton? Oh, right. That's supposed to be me.

"No broken bones. Lots of bruises, some swelling. Your leg will be sore for a few days, but you'll feel fine in about a week. Take it easy and try to rest as much as you can the next few days. I'll need to see you in a week for the stitches." He checked her chart, and before hanging it back on the end of her bed, he said, "I would release you now, but Mr. Buchanan asked that we keep you overnight."

"Mr. Buchanan?" Jessica asked.

"Yes, Kyle. Do you remember Kyle Buchanan? He's one of our local firefighters. He was the first to arrive at the scene of your accident."

Jessica felt like saying, "How could I ever forget that face, that voice!" But all she said was, "Yes, Kyle. Kyle Buchanan. I remember him."

The doctor came closer; now he sounded like a concerned father. "In reviewing your chart, I see you haven't listed an insurance carrier. Do you have any insurance, Miss Fenton? Any relatives we can contact?"

"No, I—"

"Is there anyone you know in Glenbrooke?"

"Yes, Hugh McGregor." Her words came out slurred. "He's the principal at the high school. He hired me. I'm a teacher." She found *p*'s and *m*'s especially difficult to enunciate.

The doctor adjusted his glasses and gingerly sat on the edge of Jessica's bed. "I don't suppose you've heard about Hugh yet."

Jessica imagined the worst.

"He came in two days ago, apparently with a stroke. He's in stable condition but has suffered partial paralysis. He's not able to speak at this point."

"Is he here now?" Jessica asked, trying to sit up and instantly feeling her head swim. "Can I see him?"

"He's on the second floor. I do suggest you wait until the morning, Miss Fenton. The best thing for you is rest. You have quite a lot of adjusting to do when you get out of here in the morning. The nurse will be in soon to give you something to help you sleep. Good night."

Dr. Laughlin strode to the doorway, where he stopped and turned around. He smiled sympathetically at Jessica and said, "By the way, welcome to Glenbrooke. I imagine you'll have my daughter in your class. Dawn. Dawn Laughlin. She'll be a junior this year. I'm told she's the most popular girl in school."

Jessica forced a lopsided smile and tried to nod. The way he announced this bit of news almost sounded as if he were apologizing, which made Jessica wonder what a doctor with a popular daughter would have to apologize for.

"Sleep well," Dr. Laughlin said, and vanished into the brightly lit hallway, closing the door behind him.

With the pain reliever wearing off, the brunt of her aches and bruises assaulted Jessica in the stillness of the room. But the most painful sensation of all was realizing she was by herself in a hospital bed in a strange town, and her only friend lay in bed on the floor above her, in worse shape than she.

Tomorrow morning she would be released from the hospital, and then what? Where would she go? Mr. McGregor had set up her housing for her, but if he were unable to speak, how would she find out where she was supposed to live? And if she did find the house, how would she get there? Was anything left of her car? And what about all her belongings that had been so carefully packed and wedged into the back seat and trunk?

Another fear slowly crept over her, one that overshadowed all the rest. What if, somehow, in all this, her true identity were discovered? Everything would be ruined. After all her careful planning, all her efforts to cover any tracks that would trace her to this small town tucked away in the Willamette Valley of

Oregon, could be destroyed with one tiny slip-up.

As tears began to form in her eyes, she remembered that today was her birthday. Turning her head into the stiff hospital pillow, Jessica sobbed out her fears and hurts. Never in her life had she felt so completely and painfully alone.

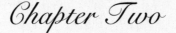

Chapter Two

*M*iss Fenton?" The morning nurse gently touched Jessica's arm. "I need to take your temperature now."Jessica rolled over and tried to focus on the woman standing by the bed. Then it all came back. The accident, the hospital, the stitches in her lip, and Kyle.

Funny that I should think of him. Jessica adjusted herself so the nurse could perform her duties.

"What time is it?" Jessica asked.

"Almost eight o'clock. You can go after the doctor sees you. Would you like some breakfast?"

"I guess. Sure." Jessica thought of her bloody clothes and wondered where they were. She didn't remember putting on the hospital gown.

The nurse finished taking Jessica's blood pressure and marking the results on the chart. She then slipped out of the room and returned a short time later with a breakfast tray. Oatmeal, orange juice, and toast.

Jessica managed to take a few bites and decided it could be worse. She wasn't sure how, but it could be.

As soon as the doctor on duty gave Jessica a quick check, the nurse opened a small closet door in the corner of the room and produced Jessica's soiled clothes.

"I wish I had something else to wear. By any chance is there a shower around here?" Jessica's first few steps were wobbly, and she felt light-headed, but she still had enough medication in her to numb the pain and get her through a quick shower. She emerged from the bathroom wearing her jeans and soiled T-shirt. She wished she had more to work with—even just her purse would help so she could brush her wet hair.

When she stepped back into her room, she heard a deep voice say, "Good morning." Kyle sat in the corner chair by the window. On the bed was her purse and an extra-large white T-shirt with red letters announcing, "Eleventh Annual Glenbrooke Firefighters' Pancake Breakfast."

"We had a couple extras down at the station. I thought you might like something clean to wear." Kyle smiled at Jessica, and she thought he looked like a shy boy. Quite a different expression from the one he had worn yesterday in the midst of the emergency.

"Thanks. I…I really appreciate it. This shirt is a mess."

"How are you feeling?"

"Better. Kind of shaky. You were really thoughtful to bring my purse and everything." Jessica reached for her purse and the T-shirt, fully aware of how ridiculous she must look in a blood-stained shirt, with stitches in her lip and her long hair dripping on the floor. "I'll be right back."

Ducking into the bathroom, she noticed her hand was shaking. She wasn't sure if it was the shock of the accident or the medication or perhaps the surprise of Kyle's sudden presence. Why would he come back unless he was interested in her?

Jessica quickly brushed her hair and pulled out the small makeup kit in her purse. Looking in the mirror, with mascara tube in hand, she realized makeup was pointless. Her lip, still swollen, looked like something from a monster movie—all distorted, with the stitches sticking out along the top. Both her eyes had red, spider-web fingers radiating from the green center, and dark shadows ran along the lower lids. Her normally peachy complexion had taken on a gray-green tone in the fluorescent light of the small bathroom.

In many ways, she looked like a different woman from her appearance a week ago. And maybe she was.

"Forget it," she muttered, jamming the wand back into the mascara tube. It wasn't like her to go out in public without wearing makeup. It also wasn't like her to don a T-shirt that advertised a pancake breakfast.

But she was in Oregon now. She wasn't the same person. Everything was going to be different.

Jessica opened the bathroom door and tried her best to look dignified. "Thanks again for bringing my purse. And I haven't thanked you yet for everything you did yesterday. I really appreciate it."

Kyle's smile hinted at his shyness again. "Don't mention it. I came back because I thought maybe you could use a ride somewhere."

Jessica sat down on the bed, suddenly feeling exhausted at the thought of all that lay before her that day. She decided to tell Kyle about Mr. McGregor, her job at the high school, and how she didn't know where her new house was. She felt vulnerable, but she carefully guarded her words. "I'd like to go upstairs to see Mr. McGregor. If he can't talk, then I guess…I guess…I'm not sure what I'll do next."

Kyle rose and came over to where Jessica sat. He spoke kindly and calmly, as he had when he'd found her the previous day. "I heard you mention his name yesterday in the emergency room so I checked on him already this morning. Hugh's in stable condition but not doing real well. His wife died a couple years ago, you know. So I took the liberty of calling on his neighbor, Ida Dane. It turns out the house he arranged for you to rent belongs to her."

"You know Mr. McGregor?" Jessica asked.

"Small town," Kyle replied. He stuck his hand in his pocket and pulled out a key, which he held in front of Jessica. "I have the key. I hope you don't mind."

Jessica didn't know if she minded or not. Of course, the key and the name of the owner of the house she would live in solved a huge mystery for her. The other mystery, Kyle, seemed more perplexing. She wanted to say, "Why are you being so nice to me? Especially right now when I look like such a mess."

Like her mother, Jessica's hair was light blond. For years she had worn it long—past the middle of her back. Then, on her way out of town two days ago, she had stopped and had it cut to her shoulders at the first hair salon she came to.

Her eyes were a mossy green, which she personally liked but didn't think were anything all that special. Her teeth were straight, thanks to three years of braces. And her figure was, in her opinion, ordinary. Not too skinny, not too heavy.

Why would Kyle be interested in her? He certainly hadn't seen her at her best. Could it be Glenbrooke suffered from a severe shortage of women? Or was this guy some kind of mass murderer?

"So," Jessica began cautiously, "do you know where the house is?"

"Marigold Lane. It's not far from the high school. About four blocks, I'd guess. Do you want me to take you there?"

"Look, you're being very nice, Kyle, but really, you don't have to do this for me."

Kyle lowered his eyes and looked at the polished hospital room floor as if he might find his next line written on a cue card there. Jessica noticed how wavy his dark hair was. He looked up, his green eyes meeting hers. "I just thought I could help out, you being new to the area and the accident and everything. If you're not comfortable with that, I understand. I'd be glad to do whatever I can for you. Just let me know, okay?" He placed the house key on the bed and walked toward the door.

"Wait," Jessica said.

Kyle stopped and turned, waiting for Jessica to speak.

"Everything is coming at me so fast. People just aren't nice like this where I come from. I could use your help. Probably more than I realize."

A grin spread across Kyle's firm jaw. "Good. Let's pay your hotel bill here and then get on over to Al's Auto Body Shop."

"Al's?" Jessica questioned.

"That's where they towed your car. We can pick up your boxes and see if by some miracle Al was able to put your Humpty Dumpty back together again."

Jessica slung her purse over her shoulder and began to head for the door, her legs cooperating stiffly. "You think it's that bad, huh?"

Kyle nodded. A wheelchair stood in the corner of the room, and Kyle positioned himself behind it, hands on the grips, indicating Jessica should get in it.

"That's okay, I can walk."

"I'm afraid this is one of those hospital policies. Nobody leaves under his—or her—own power."

"That's ridiculous! I can walk just fine."

Kyle didn't budge. His no-nonsense jaw was joined by a no-nonsense look in his eyes. Obviously he was unwilling to leave the hospital without Jessica in that wheelchair and him at the helm. Jessica found it difficult to give in. But she didn't see any other choice.

Lowering herself into the chair, she plopped her purse on her lap and refused to look at anyone as Kyle wheeled her down the hall.

He leaned over and spoke quietly to her as they made their way to the front door. "You were asking about your car. I think we should wait for Al's diagnosis, but I'm afraid it didn't look too good last night when they brought it in."

"You were there when they took my car in?" Again Jessica had uneasy feelings about this man being so involved in the details of her life. In her experience, everything had a price, especially charity.

"I stopped by when I left the hospital last night. I had to get a ride back to the site of the accident so I could pick up my truck, and I knew Al would give me a lift. Besides, you said something to Betty about needing your purse, so I thought I'd bring it to you."

"Again, thanks. Do you think we could stop by and see Mr. McGregor?"

"It's up to you. Like I said, he's not in very good shape. He certainly wouldn't recognize you or know you're in the room. If you want me to, I'd be glad to go with you."

"I guess I'll do what you suggested: Settle my account with Betty, then take care of my car. Maybe I can come back this afternoon and see him, after I move in."

She didn't make it back that afternoon, though. Al told her that her car was totaled. "Take the insurance money and don't look back," he counseled her.

Jessica nodded and left with Kyle, numbed by the news. There was one slight problem. Jessica had no car insurance.

She had planned to buy it with her first teaching paycheck. It just hadn't seemed necessary to deal with insurance immediately when she bought the car. The woman who had sold it to Jessica was willing to take cash and let Jessica drive it away right then, and that's what Jessica cared about most at that moment.

She had known she would have to obtain Oregon license plates and figured she would buy insurance at the same time. Now she realized how foolish that assumption had been. Worse, it was probably illegal, now that she thought about it. Perhaps this whole adventure was a foolish idea.

Jessica had been raised to believe that she could accomplish whatever she set out to do. "If you can dream it, you can do it" had been the slogan she had lived by since reading it off one of her roommate's posters her first year of college. Now she seriously doubted that philosophy. Expectations can become painfully dangerous when destiny is messed with by unseen, unfair forces.

Kyle loaded up the back of his white truck with her smashed boxes and drove her to 226 Marigold Lane. Jessica maintained silence the whole way, wondering if she had made the right decision in coming. Nothing was going the way she had thought it would. Perhaps this wasn't her destiny, her dream, the way she had thought it would be.

Everything changed when she saw the house. The yellow clapboard cottage with a red brick chimney took her breath away.

"This is my house?" she asked as Kyle parked the truck at the curb, right next to a huge elm tree.

"Yep. This is a great neighborhood, too. Most of the houses on this street are between seventy and one hundred years old. I used to…," Kyle paused. "I knew someone who lived on the next street over. It's a good neighborhood," he added quickly.

Jessica stepped out of the cab of Kyle's truck and stood before the charming home, scanning the trellis of pink roses growing over the front door, the stone walkway, and white shutters. Now *this* is what she had expected to find in Glenbrooke. A real, live, storybook house.

When the key clicked in the lock on the front door, Jessica opened it with Kyle right behind her. She felt as if she might be getting her second wind, another chance for this little dream of hers to survive.

The morning sun entered the house with them through the open front door. Hundreds of tiny dust fairies rose from their vacant-house hibernation and danced silently for Jessica on the polished wood floor.

"It's beautiful," she said. "I can't believe Mr. McGregor found such a great house for me! This must be the kitchen."

Straight ahead was the small but adequate kitchen, complete with a refrigerator. A door at the back of the kitchen, on the left, led to the back yard, which had a wooden deck with a few pieces of lawn furniture and the dying remains of a garden along the back fence. She noticed that all the neighbors kept their small yards neat and trimmed, and each had a garden.

Inside the house, on the left side of the kitchen, two doors led to a rectangular, open area that looked as if it served as the all-purpose dining room, living room, and office space. A hunter green couch, an oak coffee table, and a small television set on top of a bookcase filled the living room area at the front of the house. The walls were white with thick wood trim above the doors and windows. Slatted white shades were drawn open at the front window, and lace curtains hung on either side. A matching window in the dining area wore the same window treatment. Jessica liked it all. It was white and fresh and open.

The dining room table looked like the common garage sale variety. While serviceable, a tablecloth and vase of flowers in the center would definitely perk it up.

The treasure of the room was an old mahogany secretary

in the far corner, which came with a straight-back chair covered with a flowered needlepoint seat. The room looked like something out of a magazine, especially the way the sunshine came slicing through the front window and made the beveled glass on the secretary shimmer. A tablecloth, some fresh flowers, maybe a few of her antique poetry books on the shelves behind the glass secretary cupboard, and this room would match the one Jessica had dreamed of.

"It's really wonderful," she said, enjoying the exploration of her new home, yet aware that Kyle was quietly taking each step with her.

"The bathroom and bedroom must be upstairs," Kyle said. "Why don't I start hauling the boxes in while you check it out?"

She appreciated the chance to see the upstairs on her own and took the fourteen winding stairs slowly, favoring her bruised leg. The bedroom was to the left, positioned over the front entryway.

An old oak dresser with an oval mirror stood against the wall by the closet door, and on the opposite side was an antique white wrought iron bed with a patchwork comforter and an old barrel top trunk at the foot. A small oak bed stand stood by the bed. A quaint brass lamp with a stained glass shade was atop the bed stand. Two windows looked out on the street and were framed with the same wide trim, slatted shades, and lace curtains as the windows below in the living room.

Jessica walked over and opened the shades to let some fresh air into the slightly musty smelling room. She watched Kyle taking determined steps to the truck, scooping up two boxes at a time and carrying them back to her front door.

Why is he doing this? Nobody is this nice without having a motive. Can I trust him? Have I told him too much already? What if he looked in my purse and found my driver's license? Does he know that my real last name is Morgan and not Fenton?

"Would you like me to carry these suitcases upstairs for you?" Kyle called from down in the entryway.

"Sure. And there's another box marked 'closet' that needs to come up, too, if you don't mind." Jessica stood aside as Kyle stomped up the stairs, lugging the heavy bags into her new bedroom. He stopped and gave the room an approving glance.

She wanted to say to him, "Isn't it darling?" but she hesitated, not willing to be so chatty about her bedroom with this man she barely knew. "You can put them over there," she said as coolly as if Kyle were a bellhop.

He obliged without a word and tromped downstairs to bring in the rest. When he walked into the bedroom again, carrying the box and her garment bag, the strap from the garment bag caught on his watch. He put down the box and wrestled with the strap.

That's when Jessica spotted the luggage tag only inches from Kyle's hand. It still had her old address and "Jessica Grace Morgan" in gold letters across the top.

Jessica held her breath as Kyle unfastened the strap and laid the garment bag across her bed.

"Do you want some help unpacking?"

He hadn't noticed—or had he? "Uh, no. Thanks. That's okay. I can get it."

Kyle ran his fingers through his thick, dark hair and ventured another question. "Are you hungry? Do you want to get a hamburger or something?"

"No, I'm fine. Thanks."

Now Kyle looked shy again. "Do you need a ride anywhere? Did you want to go back to the hospital to see Hugh?"

"Actually," Jessica answered, remaining cautious, "I'm feeling kind of tired. I think I'll unpack a little and maybe take a nap."

Kyle leaned against the frame of the bedroom door. He seemed to fill the entire space. "Well, I guess I'll be going then. If you need anything," he paused until she looked up and met his gaze, "anything at all, just call. You can reach me at the fire station, and if I'm not there, the other guys pretty much know where I am."

Jessica nodded and looked away. He was too gorgeous. Not just his appearance, but everything about him was appealing. Each time she met his gaze she had to brace herself for the inevitable blush that raced across her cheeks.

"Well, again, thanks," Jessica said. "It seems that's all I've been saying to you—thank you, thank you, thank you." She glanced down at her T-shirt. "Oh, and I'll get the shirt back to you."

"No need. You can keep it. Actually, this year it'll be our *fifteenth* annual pancake breakfast. If you keep that eleventh annual for a few more years, it might be worth something. A real collectable."

Jessica forced herself to look up and smile. A searing pain shot through her upper lip, reminding her it was time for her medication.

"Well, I won't keep you," Kyle said, running his right thumb and forefinger across his jawline. He lifted his forefinger and tapped his closed lips. "Feel free to call me if you need anything, okay?"

"Okay. Thanks."

"You don't have to come downstairs. I'll see myself out. I hope you feel better soon."

"I will. Bye. Thanks again."

Jessica stood in place, listening for the front door to close. As soon as it did, she peeked through the window and watched Kyle walk to his truck and drive off. Then she gingerly lay down on her bed and heaved a deep sigh.

I'm dreaming. That's what all this is. A long, bizarre dream. Kyle can't be real. Men like him simply don't exist, so I must be dreaming. I'm going to close my eyes, and when I open them, none of this will have happened, and I will be back in California.

But that, Jessica decided, would definitely be a nightmare. No way could she have stayed. And no way was she going back.

She reached across the bed and unsnapped the luggage tag from her garment bag. She was in Oregon now. This is where she belonged. She removed the insert card with her name on it and tore the card into tiny pieces. She would have to be more careful, that's all. Much more careful.

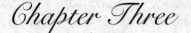

Chapter Three

The day slipped quickly into evening, and Jessica slept through it all, nestled on her bed with the patchwork comforter pulled up to her chin. When she finally awoke, it was dusk.

She stumbled to the bathroom, smiling when she noticed the quaint claw foot tub and pedestal sink. The window had one brass center latch in the middle of the two panes. Snow White would open this kind of window on a summer day, and all the little bluebirds would fly over to sit on the sill and sing with her.

Jessica debated if she should take more medication or try to find something to eat. The medicine obviously made her sleepy, which seemed good, but her stomach was beginning to complain that the few bites of morning oatmeal were long gone.

Taking the stairs slowly, her left leg feeling wobbly and undependable, Jessica padded into the kitchen to see if any food might be found. If not, she didn't know what she would do. She had no transportation, no way of even knowing which direction to walk to find the nearest store or restaurant. That is, if her legs would let her walk far enough to find food. She felt like a rather pathetic pioneer.

The refrigerator was empty. One cupboard held a set of four white plates, bowls, cups, saucers, and salad plates. In the other cupboards she found just enough mixing bowls, pots, pans, and cookie sheets to make it a ready-to-use kitchen. A cordless telephone, a half roll of paper towels, a coffee maker, and a blender rounded out the kitchen's accessories. Food was the only item missing.

One more shelf remained that she hadn't checked, a small one above the refrigerator. When she opened it, Jessica thought she spotted something back in the corner. Dragging a chair in from the dining room, she balanced herself on it so she could see inside the cupboard. To her delight, she found booty—two bags of Ramen noodles and four Lipton tea bags.

She had never eaten Top Ramen before, let alone tried to fix it. Still, it was better than nothing.

Within twenty minutes Jessica had prepared and con-sumed half a bag of noodles, taken her medication, found her pajamas, changed into them, and crawled back into bed. She had no idea what time it was but made a mental note that, when she woke up in the morning, she would unpack her alarm clock. Those were her final thoughts until nearly noon the next day.

She awoke with a pounding headache. She had slept well—hard and deep. But now her neck and head ached as if she had tried to sleep on a long airplane ride like on her last trip to England. *Maybe I better start unpacking the bathroom things first so I can find some aspirin.*

Jessica made her way slowly to the bathroom. *Funny, my lip hardly hurts anymore, and my leg feels a little better. Or is it just that my neck is so sore I don't notice the rest of me?*

Before she could find the aspirin bottle, the doorbell rang. She wondered if she should ignore it. She was still in her pajamas. It rang again, twice this time. What if it was Kyle? Jessica fumbled through her luggage to find a robe and hobbled down the stairs.

"I'm coming," she called out on the fourth ring. She unlocked the door and opened it, expecting to see Kyle.

An older woman stood on the doorstep. Her silver-rimmed glasses matched her silver-white hair. She was wearing a purple pansy on the collar of her sweater and held out to Jessica a vase full of the same.

"Welcome! I'm Ida. Ida Dane. I see Kyle helped you move. Did you find everything all right?" The woman reminded Jessica of an older version of Harriet Nelson.

"Yes, thank you. Please come in," Jessica said. "I must apologize for my appearance."

"Oh, you poor dear! Don't even think about it. Kyle told me about the accident. What a miserable way to start off here in Glenbrooke. I do hope you're feeling better. Here, these are for you." She handed Jessica the vase bubbling over with pansies.

"Thank you. They're beautiful. Yes, I am feeling a little better, except for a kink in my neck." The two women made their way into the living room and sat on the couch. Jessica placed the vase on the coffee table.

"You know," Ida said, "maybe I'll just grab a paper towel to place under that. You sit. I'll be right back."

Jessica liked Mrs. Dane immediately. Yet she felt awkward inviting someone into her home when it really wasn't *her* home but the guest's, and the guest-owner was apparently more concerned about the furniture than Jessica was. She hoped Ida wouldn't think this was an indication Jessica wasn't going to take care of things properly.

"There," Ida said, folding a paper towel twice to form a thick coaster for under the vase. "That will work just fine. I wanted to make sure you knew the trash and water are included in the rent, and I've switched the phone over to your name as well as the power bill."

"Thank you so much. The house is lovely, and I know I'm going to enjoy living here."

As if satisfied that the business side of their conversation was complete, Ida moved on to other topics. "So, you say you have a sore neck. Do you know, my son just happens to be a chiropractor. He's absolutely the best! His wife, Becky, is the sweetest thing. Why, she'll give you a massage that'll take that knot right out of there! Why don't I call them right now and make an appointment?"

"Really, that's all right. I'm not even dressed yet." Jessica wasn't sure how she felt about going to a chiropractor. The experience would be new for her and no doubt an expensive one.

When she had paid her hospital bill yesterday, she had used up all her funds except for twelve dollars and some change in her purse. She certainly hadn't thought through her financial situation before taking off. She had no possibility of coming up with more money until after her first paycheck, which probably would be two or three weeks away. The reality of her financial situation had sunk in, and she realized she was in a horrible mess. How was she going to buy food, let alone pay for a chiropractor?

"Mrs. Dane, I'm afraid I can't—"

Ida waved her to silence and spoke cheerfully into the phone. "Becky, dear, I have a new patient for you, and I wanted to know if I could bring her right over. She's my tenant at the old house on Marigold. Her name is Jessica Morgan."

Morgan! Jessica froze. Mr. McGregor had given her real name to Mrs. Dane, and now somebody named Becky at the chiropractor's office knew it, too.

"In twenty minutes? Perfect. See you then, dear." Ida hung up and turned to Jessica with a thumbs up sign. "Get dressed, Jessica dear, and we'll go right over."

"You're awfully kind, but I can't, I mean I don't…." Jessica wasn't sure what to say. She had never been out of money before. In the past, a drive through her bank ATM would replenish her money supply. Now she had no checking account to draw from and no ATM to drive through. The realization was numbing, and she didn't know how to explain this—especially to the owner of her home, who might change her mind about renting this cottage to Jessica if she knew the truth.

"Go on now. No excuses! Do you need any help upstairs?"

Jessica gave up. "No, I'll be down in a few minutes." She decided she could always stall. She could leave her purse at the house and tell the chiropractor she didn't have any money with her. Then she could ask if he would bill her.

Dressing took longer than she expected. Pulling on her jeans and slipping on her favorite blue Eddie Bauer shirt over her stiff neck took considerable effort. Now her head was really pounding. Maybe, if this chiropractor actually helped, it would be better than living in misery for days. Jessica pulled on her huaraches and spent a few minutes in the bathroom with a brush. Once again, the effort to apply makeup seemed pointless. She emerged at the bottom of the stairs with a weak smile, feeling slightly faint.

"You poor dear," Ida said, waiting by the front door. "I just realized you probably don't have a bit of food in the house. You must be starving. Why don't we stop for lunch afterwards? My treat. You can tell me all about yourself. Hugh told me so little about you."

Jessica allowed this sweet woman, who bordered on the side of busybody, to drive her to the chiropractor's office, where Jessica went through a series of X-rays followed by a consultation. Dr. Dane showed her where the accident had jarred her spine out of alignment and recommended a series of adjustments and massages beginning with three office visits a week.

In the privacy of his closed office, Jessica tried to find the words to graciously turn down his recommendation. "I must be direct, Dr. Dane. I don't have any insurance, and at this time I'm afraid I can't pay for the services up front. Perhaps I can begin the treatment after school starts, once I've received my first paycheck."

Dr. Dane looked thoughtful before closing her file on his desk. "You definitely need the treatment now. The problem will only persist and most likely will become worse the longer we wait. Why don't we call your first month of treatment my little gift to welcome you to Glenbrooke?"

Once again, Jessica was caught off-guard by the generosity of another Glenbrooke resident. "If you're sure that's okay. I feel that's an awful lot for you to do. You don't even know me."

"Accidents can cause lifelong spinal problems. As a doctor, I feel better about attending to your back right away. Let's put you on a table, and Becky can start your massage."

"Thank you, Dr. Dane. I appreciate this very much."

As Jessica lay flat on her stomach on a rather comfortable, padded table, Becky worked on Jessica's back with a low-humming massage machine. Jessica felt the tension begin to drain from her muscles. She thought about Dr. Dane and wondered if such generosity was the way of life for the people in this small, friendly town.

Perhaps all her suspicions about Kyle were unfounded. Maybe he was only doing for her what any Glenbrooke firefighter would do for someone he rescued from an accident. The thought was comforting and a little disappointing at the same time. She had almost convinced herself he was interested in her. After the massage and adjustment, Jessica felt a definite improvement.

Mrs. Dane drove to a little diner called the Wallflower, so named for its decor. Planters were built into the walls both inside and outside the restaurant, and from each planter spilled bright waterfalls of late summer flowers.

"Aren't the mums wonderful?" Ida asked as they found a corner table next to a planter of bright yellow mums. "This is my favorite little spot."

Jessica guessed that Ida loved flowers. Her front yard was probably filled with a wide variety. The topic of flowers proved to be safe ground for conversation, as Jessica worked on her sandwich, trying diligently not to bite into her still swollen top lip. She couldn't believe how much better she felt, not only from the food, but also from the massage and adjustment.

"Will you just listen to me," Ida said merrily when they arrived back at Jessica's front door. "Here I wanted to learn all about you, and instead, I yapped about myself the whole time. We'll have to go out to lunch again real soon. When do you start school?"

"Monday, I believe."

"Why, that's only two days away! You arrived just in time."

"We have teachers' meetings for a week, and then school starts the next Tuesday, right after Labor Day."

"Oh, yes, of course. Say, I'm planning to visit Hugh tomorrow morning at ten. Would you like to join me? He supposedly doesn't know anyone is in the room, but I believe he'll come around soon. The more we parade our familiar faces and voices through his room, the more it will help him. That's what I believe."

"Sure. I'd love to go with you."

The next morning at 10:15 Jessica sat in a straight-backed chair at Mr. McGregor's bedside and shyly reached over to hold his hand and give it a little squeeze. His hairline had receded far past where she remembered it to be when she last saw him, six or seven years ago. And what little hair he did have was all gray. His round face looked ashen.

"Well, I made it here, Mr. McGregor. It's Jessica Mor…," She paused and was about to say, "Fenton," but then she realized Mrs. Dane was right there, and she knew her as Jessica Morgan. "It's me, Jessica," she said quickly. "I arrived a few days ago. The house you found for me is perfect. I really like it." Jessica looked over at Mrs. Dane, who gave her an approving nod and smile.

"I took her to see Dale." Ida stepped into the one-sided conversation. "What Jessica isn't telling you is that she had an accident on the way into town."

Jessica cringed. The last thing she thought Mr. McGregor needed to hear about was her accident. The poor man had enough of his own troubles. "I'm really okay though," Jessica told him. "It wasn't bad. I did spend my first night in Glenbrooke here at the hospital. Isn't that funny? We both were in the same building, only I was downstairs."

It seemed for an instant that Mr. McGregor's eyelids fluttered. Both women moved closer, hoping he would open his eyes and start to talk as if nothing had ever happened to him. That's how it seemed it should be since he only looked as if he were taking a nap.

"So, when are you going to come home, Hugh?" Ida asked. "I sent Wendel over to mow your lawn yesterday. It was beginning to look like a jungle over there. We didn't want your yard to bring down the value of the rest of the neighborhood, you know. Thought we should keep up the place. I will have you know, however, that you can't expect to be spoiled like that much longer. You need to come home now and keep up with your own chores."

Jessica wasn't sure that Ida's prattling was helping any, but it did seem that Mr. McGregor's eyes were moving under his eyelids, which was something they hadn't been doing before. Ida had stopped talking, and the only sound was the steady beeping of the monitors, indicating electronically that life remained in Mr. McGregor, even though for the moment he was dormant.

"Well, we had better be going now," Ida said after she had chattered for nearly forty minutes. "I'll be back around to see you on Monday, if you're still here, that is. Oh, say, you really should try to get out of here today, Hugh. You know how you've been promising to come to church with us one of these days—well, tomorrow is the first Sunday for our new pastor. He's from California, but I think we're going to like him anyway. Sure wish you were going to be joining us."

Jessica gave Mr. McGregor's hand a squeeze, Ida kissed him on the cheek, and the two women left. In the car on the way home, Ida extended the Sunday-go-to-meetin' invitation to Jessica as well. According to Ida, her church was the best in town.

"Thanks, but I really need to settle in and try to regain my strength," Jessica replied, hoping that being Mrs. Dane's tenant didn't automatically mean she would be expected to attend all of Mrs. Dane's suggested meetings.

Church hadn't been part of Jessica's life since she was eight. She didn't intend to start going now. Her mother had been the spiritual influence in the family, and when she had died in the middle of Jessica's second-grade year, Jessica and the rest of the family found it difficult to continue a friendly acquaintance with a God who would let a woman like Carol Morgan die. As Jessica saw it, as long as she lived a good, moral life, God wouldn't bother her, and she saw little reason to be bothering him. After all, he had wars and starvation and global warming to worry about. He didn't need to be bothered with her petty whims.

Ida seemed to assume Jessica had visited the grocery store since yesterday, because she said something about did Jessica enjoy cooking for herself now that she was settled and could she find everything okay in the kitchen. Jessica replied, "Yes, everything is just fine." The truth was, Jessica was rationing her two bags of Ramen noodles. The night before she had found a Snickers bar in her purse and conservatively nibbled about a fourth of it before placing it in the refrigerator. It looked awfully sad and limp, all alone on that refrigerator shelf.

"I can understand your wanting to get yourself situated, Jessica. Once you're settled, I do hope you'll come to church with me." Mrs. Dane's tone was light and not pushy. She dropped Jessica off at her front door with another invitation for Jessica to call her if she needed anything.

The weather was so nice, and Jessica wasn't feeling too tired from the trip to the hospital, so she meandered into her backyard after Ida left. An old chaise lounge with a dirty cushion awaited her on the deck. Jessica stretched out and closed her eyes, tilting her face to the August sun. Malibu it wasn't, but it was still wonderfully soothing and relaxing.

As much as Jessica's body relaxed, her mind began to tense up. She reviewed her situation for the four hundredth time. *I have twelve dollars to my name. I have half a bag of noodles and five bites of a candy bar. I won't get paid for at least one week, maybe two. I don't know anyone I can borrow money from, plus I'd be too embarrassed to ever do that. Kyle said he would help me out, but then I haven't heard from him since he dropped me off here on Thursday.*

I have no car. No money to buy a car. Why didn't I plan to bring more money with me? What was I thinking? Was I thinking? How am I going to pull all this off? At least my next rent payment isn't due until October first. What about the phone? And the electricity? How am I going to do this? I've never been in debt in my life!

I can't go back now. I have to make this work!

Jessica felt exhausted over all her troubles. She tried to sleep in the warm sun, but her brain wouldn't stop long enough to let her. She tried to walk off some of her tension. The garden toward the back looked brown and ready to be torn out. The thought of yard work appealed to her, even though her leg was still sore. At least the physical labor would burn off her mental energy.

Jessica carefully knelt down and began to pull out the dead vines and stalks. She pulled back the leaves and found a big Italian squash that seemed edible despite the drought conditions in the garden. Another, smaller one next to it had rotted on the underside, but this granddaddy looked just fine.

Jessica felt as if she had found a rare treasure. Food! She carted the zucchini into the kitchen and washed it in the sink. It was at least a foot long, having hung on past its picking time.

She wasn't sure how to prepare it. Cooking had never been a priority in her life. Maybe steamed would be good. After scanning the cupboards for some spices, she found a nearly empty container of cinnamon, a full box of baking soda, and a bottle of garlic salt. It didn't take her long to steam the pan full of sliced zucchini and garnish it with the garlic salt. She deemed it a culinary success.

Proudly carrying her bowl of zesty, steaming nutrition into her dining room, Jessica sat at the table, eager for her feast. She almost felt as if she should pray, but she didn't know what to say. The first bite entered her salivating mouth and melted against her healing tongue. It was good. Very good. She savored each bite.

Maybe I'm going to be okay after all. If I just take each day at a time, I can do this. I don't need anyone to help me out. I'll be fine by myself.

Jessica pushed herself away from the table, stretched out across the couch in the living room, and tried to reinforce all the positive messages she had just given herself. Without warning, a single salty tear dipped over the edge of her eyelid and coursed its way down her cheek. No one was there to see it. No one to guess how terrified she really was.

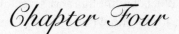

Chapter Four

"All right, teachers, if you'll find your seats, we need to start this meeting." A brusque brunette wearing a red blazer and black straight skirt pounded her hand on the podium at the front of the large meeting room.

Jessica found a seat near the back. She still felt uncomfortably conscious of the stitches in her upper lip. Actually, the morning had been fairly successful so far. She had managed to shower, dress, do an adequate job on her hair and makeup, and then walk the four blocks to the high school without feeling exhausted.

The best part was the table that had greeted her at the door with fresh coffee, a basket brimming with muffins, and a tray of fresh fruit slices. Some primal urge within her whispered that she should grab five muffins and several apples and stuff them into her purse. The day before, all she had eaten was the rest of her Snickers bar and a small bowl of steamed zucchini.

However, Jessica had managed to control herself and had

taken only one blueberry muffin and several orange wedges.
She had spoken to no one while busying herself at the table
stirring a packet of sugar and one of powdered creamer into
her Styrofoam cup of coffee.

Now, sitting by herself on the cold metal folding chair, she
sipped her coffee and glanced around the room, observing her
fellow teachers. Many of them were obviously old comrades;
they huddled together in several groups, making small talk as
if they were at a dinner party. When they found their seats, they
all sat together. Jessica felt as if it were the first day of school
and she was the new kid.

"Good morning, staff," the brunette said with a smile. "I'm
so glad to meet all of you. My name is Ms. Charlotte
Mendelson, and I am the new principal here at Glenbrooke. As
most of you know, Mr. McGregor has been hospitalized, and I
have been called on to fill his position. I come to you with
three years' experience as principal of Logan High School in
Salem."

Ms. Mendelson continued to list her accomplishments and
promised that the coming school year would be the best
Glenbrooke had ever seen. Jessica guessed her to be in her
early thirties, with a hint of a New England accent. She spoke
with cool articulation and frequent hand gestures that displayed her long red fingernails. She seemed out of place in this
small town.

"Any questions then?" Ms. Mendelson concluded after
more than an hour of speaking authoritatively from her stack
of notes. "Fine. You will find your classroom assignments listed
by the back door. I know it's going to be a wonderful year for all
of us."

Suddenly Jessica felt the cold fingers of panic creeping up
her neck. How would her name be listed? If Mr. McGregor

gave her real name to Mrs. Dane, did he list her at the school as Jessica Morgan, too?

"Oh, one more thing," Ms. Mendelson called out above the escalating noise of chairs shifting and conversations starting up. "I need to see the new English teacher." She scanned her slip of paper, "Jessica…"

Jessica moved to the front quickly, "Yes? I'm Jessica."

Ms. Mendelson scanned her up and down before replying. Her eyes rested on Jessica's lip. "I understand you are here under Hugh's personal recommendation."

Jessica nodded.

"May I ask what happened to your face?"

"I was in a car accident a few days ago."

"You're all right, I hope." It didn't sound fully sympathetic, but Jessica guessed it might be as good as it got with someone like Ms. Mendelson.

"Yes, I'm fine."

"You will have those stitches taken care of before classes start, I assume."

"I see the doctor on Wednesday." Jessica felt a mixture of anger and embarrassment.

Charlotte Mendelson seemed to be examining Jessica's lip even closer before asking, "Did they tell you it would leave a permanent scar?"

Jessica had wondered about that horrible question a hundred times during the past few days. Each time she had concluded to sweep the fear back under the carpet. How could this person pull up the rug and expose Jessica's terror like that?

"Was there something you wanted to see me about?" Jessica asked.

Charlotte pushed on, as if she were the one who had changed the subject. "It seems we don't have your file. I suppose

Hugh forwarded it to the district office already, but our secretary had only a yellow Post-It note saying, 'Jessica—English, arrive Wednesday or Thursday.'"

"Yes, that's me."

"Would you go to the office then and provide the necessary information before going to your classroom?" It was more of a demand than a question. Ms. Mendelson turned on her high red heels. She called out to a man whom Jessica guessed might be the football coach by the blue shorts he wore and the white just-a-tad-too-tight T-shirt covering his broad chest.

Jessica found her way down the hall to the office and tried to lower the temperature on the anger gauge in her head. Ms. Mendelson was someone she would have to learn to work with, and the best route might be to try to walk away from every possible conflict with her that arose.

Jessica wished she had dressed nicer for today. Instead of business attire, she had worn jeans, an ivory T-shirt, and a natural tone vest with four antique brass buttons down the front. She had pictured herself spending the day cleaning out cupboards and decorating bulletin boards, not being forced into a battle with her new boss. If she had known, she definitely would have worn the blue Liz Claiborne suit. Yes, definitely a consideration for the first day of school. Or perhaps for the first school board meeting.

When Jessica opened the door of the school office, she noticed a man with vaguely familiar broad shoulders at the counter, speaking to the school secretary.

"Could you tell me which room Miss Fenton is in?" the deep voice of Kyle Buchanan asked.

"Miss Fenton? I don't believe we have a teacher by that name," the small woman replied.

"Actually, it's me," Jessica said.

A smile spread across Kyle's face as he turned to face her.

"You're sure looking a lot better! How are you feeling, Jessica?"

The secretary peeked around Kyle's broad frame. "Oh," she said, "so you're Jessica. We didn't even have your last name written down. Fenton, is it? F-e-n…" The secretary stopped, with her pencil poised on her notepad, waiting.

"T-o-n," Jessica finished for her.

"Good. I need to ask you a few questions before you leave the office."

"I won't keep you," Kyle said. He lowered his voice and leaned closer to Jessica. His green eyes raced around her frame and face before coming to the finish line—her eyes. "I've been on duty at the station the last few days, but I have the next few off, so I thought I'd see if you needed anything. Don't you need to go back to the doctor's on Wednesday? Could you use a ride?"

Jessica was about to give her usual, "That's okay, you don't have to worry about me" answer, when Charlotte burst through the door.

"Well, hello!" she cooed the moment she saw Kyle. "I don't believe we've met yet. I'm the school principal, Charlotte Mendelson." She held out her hand, as if Kyle were expected to kiss it. Kyle politely shook it.

"Kyle Buchanan."

"By any stroke of good fortune, are you the new teacher I haven't met yet?"

"He's a firefighter," the secretary piped up from her overflowing desk. "Everyone knows Kyle."

Charlotte kept on smiling and said, "Well, a firefighter. You'll have to come and do an assembly on fire safety for me. I'm sure you're a fabulous speaker. Shall we step into my office and arrange a date?"

Jessica felt her anger toward this woman boil up inside all over again.

"Actually, I need to get going," Kyle said politely. "Anyone on our crew would be glad to help out with an assembly. You can call the fire station whenever you find a time that fits in with your schedule."

"Fine. I'll do that." Charlotte smiled at Kyle as if she could magnetize him.

He turned his attention back to Jessica. "Wednesday, then?" he asked. "I'll call you and find out what time you want me to pick you up."

Jessica nodded.

"Excuse me, ladies." Kyle nodded to each of them and left.

"How do you know him?" Charlotte asked Jessica.

Jessica considered not responding and simply walking away, but she would have to come back anyway to answer the secretary's questions. Plus, like it or not, this woman was her boss. She had been in worse situations. She could handle herself with Charlotte.

"We met on a blind curve."

"What?" Charlotte demanded.

Jessica took two steps past Charlotte and asked the secretary, "Did you need me to fill out some papers for you?"

The tiny woman behind the desk looked wide-eyed at Jessica and said, "Oh, yes, only a few forms here. We have nothing about you in our files, you see. And sometimes it takes days or even weeks to get copies from the district office. It would certainly help if you wouldn't mind filling these out for me."

"Sure. Would you like them back today, or may I bring them to you tomorrow?"

"Tomorrow would be fine," the secretary said, nodding her head.

"We need them today," Charlotte inserted into the conversation. "Until those papers are filled out, you are not officially employed at my school. Do you understand, Ms....?" Charlotte shot a sharp glance at the secretary as if Jessica were invisible. "What's her last name?"

The secretary quickly fumbled for her notepad. "Uh, Fenton. Jessica Fenton."

"Do you understand, Ms. Fenton?"

Jessica would *not* let this woman get the better of her today, tomorrow, or any day. Charlotte Mendelson would *not* control her.

Without a word, Jessica turned to the secretary and said, "Would you like me to use a pen or pencil, or does it matter?"

"Pen, of course," Charlotte barked and strode into her office, purposefully leaving the door open.

"Pen, I guess," the woman replied, handing Jessica two short forms. "And this is a school handbook. You can keep that. I guess I'll take the forms when you've completed them."

Jessica sat in a straight-backed wooden chair in the corner of the waiting area, as far away from Charlotte's door as possible. She filled out her name, address, and phone number, which she copied from a card she had placed in her purse the day before. There wasn't much else in her wallet. She had burned her Sprint FONCARD, her Bank of America Versatel card, her California driver's license, and four major credit cards. All that was left was the card she had made the night before with her hand-printed new identity and the last studio photo taken of her and her mother.

From the principal's office, Jessica heard Charlotte's speaker phone as she made a call. It rang twice, and then a male voice answered, "Glenbrooke Fire Station. This is Bobbie."

"Kyle Buchanan, please," Charlotte replied.

"Kyle's off for the next three days. Can someone else help you?"

"No, I think I'll try him at home. Say, do you happen to have that number handy?"

Jessica tried to block out the game going on in the next room. She stuck to her forms, filled them out front and back, and handed them to the secretary.

"I'll see you later," Jessica said and left as quickly as she could to hide in the safety of room 14—*her* room. She opened the door, slid inside, and leaned against the closed door while letting out a pent-up sigh.

Opening her eyes, she took in her surroundings. Plain enough, old enough, and just clean enough. Room 14 reminded Jessica of one of her old high school classrooms. The long brick buildings that housed Glenbrooke High School had to be thirty, maybe forty, years old. The room had the smell of ground-in eraser dust, and yet many improvements such as the new lighting and the white boards that replaced chalkboards made it a "modern" school.

Jessica focused in on her desk at the front of the room. Reverently she approached it and ran her hand across the wood surface, feeling each nick. She smiled contentedly to herself. While the desk was old, solid wood with an intriguing relief map of its many years etched across its surface, the chair was brand new, with black vinyl arms and a gray fabric seat. It had two levers on the side so the chair could be adjusted up and down or back and forth. Jessica tried out the high-tech gem, chuckling to herself as a pull on the first lever took her down instantly. Better not show the class clown where that lever was. But then, class clowns already know those things, don't they?

She heard a light tapping at the closed door, and then it squeaked open. Jessica immediately stood up, as if she had been caught goofing off and Charlotte was going to yell at her.

"Hi," a cheery voice called out. "Are you Jessica? I'm Teri." A medium height Hispanic woman with full, wildly curly, long brown hair entered the room. She had on a white, sleeveless, collared shirt and a baggy pair of cut-off jeans shorts. In contrast to her smooth, tanned skin and dark, snappy eyes, her white teeth shone like pearls.

Jessica met Teri halfway across the room and shook Teri's extended right hand. "I'm your neighbor," Teri said. "I teach Spanish right over there." She pointed to the back of the classroom. "I hear you're going to teach English and a health ed class. I teach one health ed class, too. This year I think they tried to split it up so all the teachers each have one class. It's not that bad. Kind of a nice break, actually. How long have you been here? Are you all settled?"

Teri fit the pattern of the friendly Glenbrooke folk. Close up, Jessica noticed that Teri didn't wear a drop of makeup, yet her skin was stunning. Jessica guessed her to be the same age as herself, but how could a twenty-five-year-old have the skin of a newborn?

Jessica told Teri how she had unpacked everything over the weekend but was a little slow at getting organized because of the car accident.

"Car accident?" Teri said. "How awful! Did the paramedics come and everything? Were you terrified?"

"A firefighter apparently saw the accident, and he stopped and radioed for help. I thought later that if he hadn't seen it, I might have lain in that ditch for hours."

"Who found you? Bobbie, Rod, Kyle, or Jim?"

"Kyle. Do you know him?"

"Of course. Everyone knows Kyle. He's the best. Really. Kyle's an incredible guy. A real knight in shining armor, you know?"

Jessica nodded, not sure if Teri meant Kyle was a knight to every woman in Glenbrooke or a knight in shining armor to Teri personally, or just an all-around great guy.

"Anyway, I'm pretty much settled in my little house, and I

go back to the doctor day after tomorrow to have these stitches taken care of." Jessica made an apologetic gesture toward her upper lip. Teri looked closer.

"Oh, I hardly noticed," Teri said. "So, what do you think? Should we work on our rooms first or go to an early lunch?"

Before Jessica could answer, Teri said, "I vote early lunch, and it's my treat. What do you think?"

"You're on," Jessica said. She grabbed her purse, and the two women headed for Teri's Volkswagen Rabbit.

Jessica felt as if she had successfully completed the unwritten, ageless entrance exam given to all new kids on the first day of school—she had made a new friend.

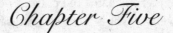

Chapter Five

*Y*our lip has healed well," Dr. Laughlin said, examining Jessica under a bright light. "However, I'm afraid we weren't able to restore you completely."

What is that supposed to mean? Where's a mirror? Let me see!

"It's only a slight scar," Dr. Laughlin continued, scrunching up his nose and peering through his bifocals. "Hardly worth mentioning. I'm afraid, short of cosmetic surgery, there's not much we can do. Won't affect you much, I imagine. Try not to think about it."

Jessica felt like crying. How could she *not* think about it when a doctor had just informed her she would be scarred for life? How dare he brush it off so lightly. This was her face they were talking about.

Before Jessica had a chance to look in the mirror, she decided she would have cosmetic surgery as soon as she could save up the money. She had turned down the school's insurance because she couldn't figure out how to come up with false medical records under the name of Fenton. She would have to save money, somehow. That is, after she had saved enough for a car. And car insurance. First, she would have to obtain an Oregon driver's license. Would they give her one with no driving record? This cover-up was becoming complicated.

"That's all then," Dr. Laughlin said, snapping off the lamp above Jessica's face and washing his hands in the stainless steel sink. "I still want you to limit your use on that left leg. Try to sit with it elevated whenever possible and don't do any strenuous exercise like aerobics, bike riding, or jogging for at least another three weeks. Okay?"

Jessica nodded. She couldn't wait for him to leave the room so she could sneak a look at her lip in the mirror above the sink. She knew Kyle would be waiting outside for her, and she wanted to see the scar before he did. Dr. Laughlin opened the door and motioned for her to exit ahead of him. She wished he had left her alone for a few minutes by herself.

"Ready?" Kyle asked, rising from the waiting room's brown plaid couch and gazing just a little too long at her upper lip. What did he think? How bad was it? She couldn't tell by the look on his face.

"I think I'll duck into the restroom, if you don't mind waiting another minute," Jessica said.

"Not a bit. I'll be right here." Kyle picked up the copy of *Time* magazine he had been reading and sat down, thumbing through it to find his place.

Jessica pushed the restroom's door open and felt relieved no one else was there. She stood at the sink and stared at her reflection in the mirror. The scar was easily seen. The whitish, half-moon shape perched half on her lip and half on her face, about a quarter of an inch from the corner of her mouth.

Jessica purposed to put her positive mental attitude into position. *It's not too bad.*

But then her negative side galloped into her thoughts. *Oh, yes, it is! It's awful. It's permanent!*

It's only temporary. I'll have cosmetic surgery just as soon as I can.

Yeah, in about fifty years when you have enough money saved up. Until then, you're going to be walking around disfigured; everyone will notice. Wherever you go, people will stare at your lip.

Jessica tried to make both sides of the war scatter from her mind. She pulled a tube of lipstick from her purse and went to work. One last look in the mirror told her the lipstick was an improvement. It covered at least half of the tiny moon, and for now, that was good enough for her.

Kyle didn't seem to notice when she joined him in the lobby. At least he didn't look at her the way he had when she first exited the doctor's office. He walked alongside her to the car, talking about an article he had just read about black holes in outer space. Jessica decided that was a good place to focus their conversations—in outer space.

Kyle had taken her to the chiropractor before her visit with Dr. Laughlin, and now he made a quick stop at Dairy Queen before returning her to school. Things became awkward at this point.

Kyle ordered for himself, then turned and said, "What would you like?"

Jessica's pride rose to the fore. "I'll get my own." She only had the twelve dollars she had been hoarding for almost a week. Not much to carry her through, but she couldn't accept Kyle's offer.

He paid for his order, and Jessica stepped up to the window and ordered a junior hamburger and a small Coke. The clerk behind the window asked if she wanted tomatoes and onions on her burger, and she hesitated, wondering if it cost more. "No, thanks," she said, pulling her money from her wallet casually and handing him a ten-dollar bill as if plenty more were stashed where that came from.

They sat at one of the picnic tables out front, Jessica with her junior burger and Kyle with his triple burger, large fries, and Oreo shiver. She had been to lunch with many men in her time and had gone dutch with many as well, but she couldn't remember ever going dutch at a Dairy Queen. And she certainly couldn't remember ever having this feeling of panic over money.

Within the first five minutes of their lunch, Jessica counted four people who greeted Kyle by name. He introduced Jessica to each of them, and once again she felt their warm Glenbrooke welcome. Of course, Kyle introduced her as Jessica Fenton.

At first, using a fake last name hadn't seemed false, but like a necessity, and she hadn't felt bad using it to protect herself. But now she felt prickly every time she heard it repeated.

Teri had invited her over to her house for dinner on Friday. How could she become close friends with Teri without revealing her true identity? And what if a possibility really existed of developing a relationship with Kyle? How could she allow herself to become close to him? Jessica Fenton must not allow anyone to get too close. She could be friendly, of course, but she could never be intimate or self-revealing the way Jessica Morgan had been.

As Jessica took another bite of her hamburger, a painful thought paraded across her mind. *Had Jessica Morgan ever been close to anyone?* Immediately she knew that, aside from her mother, the answer was no. "Morgans do not make friends," her father had once said. "Morgans network."

"I suppose we should get back to school," Kyle remarked, fishing in the bottom of his brown sack for the few final french fries. He tossed the bag and empty shiver cup into the trash can behind him. "Teri said you're scheduled for meetings all day tomorrow and Friday."

"Yes. I'm just about ready to feel overwhelmed."

"Was the first week this packed at your last school?" Kyle asked.

Jessica hesitated. "Actually, this is my first school. It's my first year of teaching anywhere. Except for my student teaching, of course."

"I'm sure you'll do fine," Kyle said.

Two teenagers pulled up in an old blue truck. They honked, called out Kyle's name, and waved.

"You seem to be pretty popular around here," Jessica teased.

"Small town," Kyle said. "You'll get honked at too, after the first couple of school days. Just wait, you'll see. We have great kids in this town."

"Have you lived here long?" Jessica asked once they were back in Kyle's truck and headed for the high school.

"About six years. I really like it here. I grew up in Portland. This small town is more my pace. How do you like Glenbrooke so far?"

"I like it. Everyone is nice and friendly. It's a lot like I thought it would be."

"Did you come from a small town in California?" Kyle asked.

"How did you know I was from California?" Jessica asked, her shields automatically going up.

"The license plates on your car. By the way, Al didn't charge you for towing your car, did he? I told him not to."

"Why?"

"Well, because..." Kyle paused.

Jessica waited for him to say, "Because I knew you didn't

have any money." She hated feeling like a charity case.

"Because I told him you were new in town, and I…" Again Kyle seemed to choose his words carefully. "I told him I'd do him a favor someday. That's how things work around here. The barter system is very much alive in Glenbrooke."

Jessica was trying to decide if she should speak up and defend herself or just let it go. How much of Kyle's kindness was part of the way of life around this town? Was he interested in her as more than a needy newcomer?

Kyle pulled into the school parking lot and turned off the engine. "I'll walk you in. I have to check on something in the office."

They walked silently as Jessica's imagination conjured up an image of Ms. Mendelson being the "something" Kyle had to check on. Charlotte had to be five, maybe six, years older than Kyle. Why would she go after him in such a big way? Jessica cast a sideways glance at Kyle, and the answer was obvious. The man was gorgeous. Not to mention kind, tender, compassionate, and understanding. Any woman would be crazy *not* to try to capture his undivided attention. Jessica felt a twinge of remorse that she had determined to hold Kyle at arm's length.

"Well, hello!" Charlotte said, appearing suddenly as the two of them stepped into the building. Jessica wondered if Charlotte's office window faced the school parking lot and she had been watching them walk into the school.

Ignoring Jessica, Charlotte sidled up to Kyle. "I see you received my messages. Let's go into my office. We have so much to discuss."

Kyle stood his ground, not budging as Charlotte pulled on his arm.

"I'll see you later," Jessica said. "Thanks a lot for the ride." Then remembering Kyle's statement about Al and the barter system, Jessica added, just for spice in front of Charlotte, "I'll have to do something nice for you someday." She headed down the hall slowly so she could hear Kyle and Charlotte's conversation.

"Bye, Jessica," Kyle said. Then he changed his tone of voice and said to Charlotte, "I can do the fire safety check you requested on the building tomorrow. I need the right forms from the station, and I didn't bring them with me today. As for the assembly, the end of the month would be the best for me."

"Wonderful," Charlotte cooed. "And what about setting a date when I can fix you dinner to thank you?"

"We'll have to wait on that," Kyle said.

Jessica couldn't hear any more as she entered her classroom. But she had heard enough to give her some hope, hope that Kyle was spending his free time with Jessica because he wanted to. Hope that there might be room for their relationship to develop into something. But what? And what would she do with it if it did?

The phone on the wall next to her desk rang, and Jessica jumped just a little before hurrying to the front of the class to answer it.

"Hi, it's Teri. I thought I heard you come in, neighbor. Is it okay if I come visit?"

"Sure, come on over."

Teri appeared a minute later. She had her wild, wavy dark brown hair back in a clip and wore a red tank top and a pair of white pants that were just a little too tight for her. Jessica noticed then that Teri's thighs were large and not at all in proportion to the rest of her figure. She had hidden her thighs well over the last few days, but today the white slacks did nothing to camouflage them.

"How did everything go at the doctor's?"

"I'm scarred for life," Jessica tried to make it sound like a joke.

"Really?" Teri came closer and looked at Jessica's lip. She did it in such a way that it seemed as if she had to look hard and long to see the scar at all. Jessica knew it was much more obvious than that, yet she appreciated Teri's benevolent act.

"It's hardly a scar at all," Teri said. "A little aloe vera and that tiny mark will heal right up. My grandma grows the plants in her back yard in Escondido. That's where I grew up. I have a dozen plants growing in my back yard. I'll bring you one tomorrow. Have you ever used an aloe plant? You just break off a leaf and put the gel right on the spot. It'll heal up in no time."

The only kind of aloe Jessica knew about came as an additive in lotion or shampoo when the manufacturer wanted it to appear to be a more natural product.

"The stuff really works. I use it on my face, too. It's kind of slimy and smells a little too earthy for me, but it's a habit. My grandma started spreading the gel on my face when I was a teen to keep it from breaking out. You'd like my grandma. She's quite a character. I can just hear her now, 'Teresa Angelina Raquel Moreno, have you used your aloe today?'" Teri rattled off the question in a high pitched, grandmotherly voice with a perfect Spanish accent.

Jessica wondered if the aloe was, in fact, the secret to Teri's flawless complexion.

Teri looked around Jessica's classroom. "It's looking good in here. Did all your books come in?"

"I'm not exactly sure. How do I find out?"

"Ask Charlotte, I guess."

"In that case, I think I'll wait."

"That bad, huh? Did she convince Kyle to do an assembly yet?"

"Yes, I heard them talking about it after Kyle brought me back. She was waiting in the hallway, all coiled and ready to spring the minute we walked in the door. It's creepy. Is she bugging you and the other teachers, too? Or is it only me?"

Before Teri could answer, Jessica's phone rang. Since Teri was standing the closest to it, she answered the call. "You're kidding! Really? That's great! Of course. We'll be right there!" She hung up and turned to Jessica, her brown eyes shining. "Guess," she challenged.

"I don't know. Charlotte just resigned."

"Better. Mr. McGregor is awake and asked to see you."

"You're kidding!"

"Of course I'm not kidding," Teri said, charging to the back of the room. "Let me grab my car keys, and we'll drive right over. This is such an answer to prayer. Thank you, Lord!"

Jessica silently agreed that it *was* an answer to a prayer. But she was surprised to hear Teri say it, especially when she added the "thank you, Lord" part.

The two women sped across town and rushed to the hospital's second floor to see Mr. McGregor. Ida greeted them at the door. She had a string of pink sweet peas draped down the right side of her yellow blouse. "Oh, good! You got my message, Jessica. Now, one at a time, girls, and speak nice and slow and clear."

Jessica went in first. She eased herself into the chair next to the bed and smiled into the dazed looking eyes of a man she once thought was the wisest man in the world. "Hi, it's me, Jessica."

"Jessica? How are you? I understand you entered Glenbrooke with fanfare." Mr. McGregor didn't sound like he was in any pain. But his expression was flat. Non-existent. It almost seemed as if some ventriloquist were pulling invisible strings attached to Hugh's eyes and lips, putting words into his mouth at the right time.

"It was rather exciting," Jessica said lightly. "I'm fine, though."

"Good. And you like the house?"

"Oh, yes," Jessica said, warming up. "It's exactly what I wanted. It's really charming. And comfortable, too. Thanks, Mr. McGregor."

"And you are safe?"

"You mean in the house? Yes, I feel very safe."

"Safe in being here?" Mr. McGregor spoke softly.

"I think so." Jessica didn't want to say anything about how Ida knew her last name, even though she was anxious to ask him whom else he had told.

"Is school okay?"

"Everyone misses you and wishes you would come back. The new principal is…, well, let's just say she doesn't seem to be out to make many friends this year."

"Your file—," Hugh began, but Ida bustled in with Teri beside her.

"All right, now," Ida said efficiently. "Your time is up, Jessica, dear. It's Teri's turn."

"Your file…," Hugh began again, but then stopped, apparently realizing that the visitors had switched positions, and it was now Teri who sat next to him.

Jessica waited outside while Teri visited with Mr. McGregor for a few minutes. *What about my file? What were you going to tell me?*

Against Ida's warnings, Jessica slipped back in after Teri left and said, "You mentioned something about my file. Is there anything I need to know?"

Hugh breathed out slowly and said, "I don't remember."

Jessica wasn't sure if he was tired and really couldn't remember or if he could only tell her in private so he held back since Teri and Ida were standing beside her.

"Well, don't worry about anything," Jessica said, trying to sound confident. "You just take it easy. I'll be back to visit you as soon as I can. And if you happen to remember what you wanted to tell me about my file, you can tell me next time, okay?"

Once the three of them slipped into the hallway, Ida spoke enthusiastically. "Isn't it wonderful? The doctor isn't predicting a full recovery yet, but he's hopeful. Would you girls like to grab a bite to eat? It's broccoli cheese soup day at the Wallflower."

"Thanks, but I've already had lunch," Teri said.

"Me, too," added Jessica. "I'm so glad you called me. I'll try to get back here to see him tomorrow or Saturday."

"Call me if you need a ride," Ida said. "Oh, and Teri, you did tell Jessica about the big church picnic on Labor Day, didn't you? Of course you're invited. You're both coming, aren't you?"

Teri turned to Jessica, suppressing a smile at Ida's brimming-over enthusiasm. "You're welcome to come."

"It's always so much fun," Ida continued. "Potato sack races, pie eating contests, and a coin toss fund-raiser. All money earned at the coin toss goes to our mission in Mexico."

"Kyle's baby," Teri said out of the side of her mouth to Jessica. Jessica had no idea what she was talking about.

"I'll see you young beauties at the picnic." Ida waved cheerfully and hurried down the hallway toward the hospital exit.

"What a sweetie," Teri said. "That woman amazes me. I hope I have that much energy when I'm eighty-two."

"You're kidding! She looks as if she's about sixty," Jessica said.

"I know. Her husband looks his age, but Wendel is just as much fun as she is. He owned the hardware store for something like fifty years." Teri led the way down the hall and back to her car in the hospital parking lot. "I wonder if Charlotte missed us while we were gone."

"Oh, please," Jessica groaned as she got in the car and

buckled up her seat belt. "Do you honestly believe she'll make it through this whole school year as principal?"

Before she could answer, Teri pulled onto Main Street. A bright yellow convertible sports car zipped past them. The teenaged girl at the steering wheel beeped her horn and waved at Teri. Teri waved back and called out, "Hi, Dawn."

"Dawn?" Jessica questioned. "Is that the doctor's daughter?"

"Yes, indeed," Teri said. "You've just seen a flash of Dawn Laughlin, Girl Wonder."

"Pretty fancy car."

"Pretty fancy girl," Teri quipped.

"Anything particular I should know about her?" Jessica asked.

"I'm not sure what I can tell you that you won't discover for yourself. She's a junior this year. Straight-A student, head cheerleader. Let's see, what else? The new car was her sixteenth birthday present last May. She spent two months in Paris with her mom this summer. Actually, her parents are divorced; she's the youngest child. The other two are married, and her mom lives in Paris. Dawn goes there every summer. Oh, and her mom is remarried to a millionaire. That's all. Just your average Glenbrooke teen."

"How does she manage to fit in with the rest of the kids?"

"She's their idol. Seems to enjoy the role, too."

Something inside Jessica went out to Dawn. She imagined a lot of expectations were placed on Dawn to be a certain kind of girl and perform her expected role, not only for her parents but also for her peers. Jessica knew that sort of pressure, and she empathized with Dawn without having met her.

"Sure is good to see Mr. McGregor recovering so well," Teri said as they drove on. She turned down a street lined with trees that formed a natural canopy. "I love this street. It's a little jog out of the way, but I take it so I can go through this tree tunnel. Wait until the fall when the leaves change. You're going to love it here! I'm glad you came to Glenbrooke."

"I am, too," Jessica said. She couldn't express to Teri or anyone else just how glad she was.

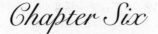

Chapter Six

*W*hen Jessica set out to walk the four blocks to school the next morning, the sun had broken through the usual early morning clouds, and she could feel its warmth on her shoulders. She hummed softly, but when she turned the corner at Maple Street, her humming received some competition. A pair of birds squawked at each other on the telephone wires over her head. *Just like my mom and dad used to argue.*

Jessica thought of Dawn and her divorced parents. *Would my parents have divorced eventually if Mom had lived?*

A squirrel darted out from under a huge hydrangea bush and skittered past Jessica on its way to the telephone pole. With the squirrel's sudden ascent, the birds flew away. Another squirrel poked its nose out from under the lavender snowball hydrangea. In a flash, he scampered up the pole, in hot pursuit of the first squirrel. Jessica imagined them to be courting. Opening the door in her mind marked "children's stories," Jessica began to unfurl mentally a story of two squirrels falling in love, cavorting together, having great adventures, and eventually raising a family of twelve baby squirrels. She decided she would title it, *Under the Flowering Bush.*

That was her secret dream, to someday write a children's storybook and to write it well enough that it would be published. Her English major had opened to her a world of authors whom she admired. For at least six years now she had kept a journal of ideas for children's books. But she had never told anyone of her dream. It was hers alone, a solitary sort of fantasy.

Her thoughts suddenly filled with an image of Kyle. Was he also some sort of fantasy? Jessica knew so little about him. He knew even less about her. And that's how she needed to keep things. Pity. If ever she longed to be pursued the way that squirrel was chased up the phone pole, it was now.

Glancing over her shoulder, Jessica scanned the phone wires down to the end of the street, looking for the playful squirrels. They were gone.

Once inside the comfort zone of room 14, Jessica set to work recording her assignments in her lesson plan book for the first two weeks of school. She had arrived a little early and was glad for the chance to finish her planning before the all-day meetings began.

A few minutes before nine o'clock, Jessica locked up her desk and headed for the meeting. More than anything else, she was looking forward to the food table, which had been bountifully stocked each day with muffins, fruit, coffee, and sometimes yogurt.

This morning Jessica took two muffins, as much fruit as she could mound up on her small paper napkin, and a carton of strawberry yogurt. She hadn't had much to eat since the hamburger and Coke with Kyle the day before at Dairy Queen.

Last night she had tried to fix the last of her foot-long zucchini by slicing it up and frying it. Without any butter or oil, the thin circles burnt horribly, and smoke had filled the kitchen. Jessica was embarrassed when the smoke detector went off. She had aired out the house, washed the frying pan, and sadly picked out the five or six slices of zucchini that were still edible. Consoling herself by splurging and using one of her two remaining Lipton tea bags to make a cup of tea, Jessica had curled up on the couch with an old book of Walter de la Mare's poems for children. She thought about how wonderful the school muffins would taste the next morning.

She was right. Before she even found a seat, she took a bite of the blueberry muffin, and it melted in her mouth.

"Jess, over here." Teri waved from the second row.

Jessica joined her, and Teri proudly presented her with a potted plant. The long, pointed leaves weren't very pretty. Something from the cactus family, Jessica guessed.

Teri must have noticed the skeptical look on Jessica's face. "It's the aloe vera plant I told you about. What did you think it was?"

"I would have guessed a Venus flytrap."

"Those have red leaves," Teri said. "Remember what I told you about this? Tear off a tip of the leaf like this and squeeze the gel out on your lip."

"Doesn't it ruin the plant?" Jessica asked, popping her last bite of blueberry muffin into her mouth.

"No, not at all. The plant heals itself."

"Kind of like a star fish," the man behind them commented, leaning forward and inviting himself into the conversation.

"Hi, Martin," Teri said without turning around. Her voice carried a cool breeze.

"And who is this?" asked the middle-aged, slim, bearded man. When neither of the women answered immediately, he jumped in with, "I'm Martin Monroe. Biology." He extended a right hand to Jessica.

"I'm Jessica," she replied, placing her cup of coffee on the floor and turning to shake his hand. It felt cool and thin. "I'm teaching English this year."

"Very nice to meet you," he said with a smile that revealed teeth with a slight gap between the front two. "Are you single gals roommates this year? You are single, aren't you?"

Jessica couldn't help but feel as if she were cornered at some cheesy bar and this Martin guy was trying out his best pick-up lines on her.

Before Jessica or Teri could answer, Charlotte stepped to the microphone and called the meeting to order. Everyone seemed to sit up a little straighter in their seats. Jessica suspected it was an involuntary reflex, not unlike the way a private would react when his sergeant marched into the barracks. She refused to respond that way to Charlotte and purposefully slumped down in her seat.

The rest of the morning dragged on as the teachers listened to instructions on everything from earthquake procedures to filling out requisition forms for materials. In Jessica's opinion, the instructions were overkill. Charlotte's apparent need for control was already beginning to have a paralyzing effect on the teachers. She glanced around and noticed blank stares replacing the previously lively expressions on the teachers' faces.

Once again, Jessica refused to be manipulated. She flipped over the page in her handbook and on the back side wrote, *Under the Flowering Bush.* She then jotted down possible names for her little squirrels. Frank and Maude? Mac and Melanie? Puffy and Fluffy?

Soon half the page was filled, and she had no idea what Charlotte had been droning on about. There was a pause and Charlotte said, "We'll break now for lunch. I've had it catered, and I see they're ready for us in the back of the room. Please try to eat quickly. We're only breaking for half an hour."

Jessica and Teri filed into line with the rest of the sleepy-eyed teachers. Again, Jessica wasn't shy about filling her plate. The stacked deli tray and potato salad looked delicious to her, especially since all she had left at home was less than half a bag of Ramen noodles and one tea bag.

Teri and Jessica stepped outside to eat their lunch standing up. The change of position felt good. Teri lowered her head and closed her eyes while standing frozen in place. It looked to Jessica as if Teri had become dizzy and was trying to regain her equilibrium.

"Are you okay?" Jessica asked, tilting her head and trying to peer at Teri's closed eyes.

Teri raised her eyelids slowly. A smile crept up her face. "I was praying," she said softly.

"Oh, I'm so sorry! I didn't know. I thought…. Never mind. Go ahead. I hope I didn't interrupt you or anything."

Teri laughed at Jessica's apologetic words and said, "It's okay, Jess. And don't worry. I put in a good word for you, too."

Now Jessica laughed, but Teri didn't.

Strange girl, Jessica thought. *I don't think I've ever known anyone who prayed in public. I wonder if Charlotte will go over those rules this afternoon. "Regulations Regarding the Rights of Teachers to Pray Before Lunch."*

Jessica took a big bite of potato salad. From behind her came Charlotte Mendelson's voice. "Well, I see one of us doesn't see the need to diet."

Forcing the rest of the spoonful of potato salad into her mouth, Jessica began to chew and declined to answer. She did notice that Charlotte seemed to parade her can of Slim Fast past Jessica as the principal moved on to the next gathering of teachers and announced, "Twenty more minutes, staff."

Jessica and Teri exchanged unspoken words with their expressive eyes and continued to eat their lunches. Before they had finished, Martin joined them and started up his "what's your sign, baby" style of jargon again.

"Will you please excuse us?" Teri asked before he had gotten any kind of response from either of them. "We need to make a run to the little girls' room before the meeting begins."

Jessica followed her cue and walked with Teri down the hall to the faculty restroom. Half of her sandwich and a few more bites of potato salad were still on Jessica's plate. Actually, her stomach must have shrunk in the past week due to her limited diet, and she found it hard to imagine how she was going to stuff the rest of the food into her mouth. But she couldn't bring herself to throw away the food. Once they were inside the restroom, she decided to wrap the sandwich in a paper towel and stick it in her purse. She felt like a neurotic miser, but did it anyway.

"I suppose I don't need to tell you to beware of Martin the Masher," Teri whispered once they were safe behind the bathroom doors.

"He is something else," Jessica said. "He reminds me of a mad scientist who experimented with lizards all his life and somehow got his molecules mixed up with theirs." Jessica gave a little shiver. "Is he creepy but harmless? Or does he eat flies and slide under rocks when no one is looking?"

"I don't know. I try to keep my distance."

"To be on the safe side," Jessica suggested, "why don't we move our seats before the next round of meetings begins? I'll feel a little better without him breathing down my neck."

"Good idea," Teri agreed.

They sat in the back this time, which gave them a little more room to nod off without being noticed. Jessica felt certain all the information they were covering was listed in the handbook and stack of orientation papers they had been handed the first day. She had skimmed the material already and had found little reason for Charlotte to have to repeat everything.

After several hours of reviewing the information, Ms. Mendelson stopped mid-sentence and stared at the back door. Jessica looked over her shoulder. Kyle stood there in his firefighter uniform. She didn't expect her heart to begin racing, but it did.

Kyle looked at Jessica and smiled.

"I don't believe it," Teri whispered when her eyes followed the trail of Kyle's smile, and it landed on Jessica.

"What?" Jessica whispered back.

"Nothing."

Charlotte found her voice and instructed her staff to take a ten-minute break. She hurried to greet Kyle at the back door. Jessica stood and turned around, pretending to be stretching, but really trying to get a clear view of Kyle and Charlotte. Kyle lifted his clipboard and pointed with his pencil at the ceiling. Jessica guessed he must be in the middle of the fire inspection Charlotte had requested. So why did he need to consult with her?

"Very interesting," Teri said softly.

"What?" Jessica asked, sitting back down and scanning Teri's face.

Teri folded her arms across her chest, and tilting her head, she looked at Jessica as if seeing her in a brand new light. "I never would have guessed," was all she said.

"Guessed what?" Jessica wanted to grab Teri by the shoulders and shake her so she would spill the mystery beans.

"Kyle told me last week that he had met somebody. I never guessed it was you."

"What do you mean it's me? He didn't meet me. He rescued me. He must have been telling you about someone else."

Teri shook her head. "Like who? Charlotte, maybe? I don't think so, Jessica. Kyle didn't tell me who it was, but after that smile he just gave you, I know it's you."

Jessica felt the insides of her stomach begin to flutter. She had to put an end to this right now. "Teri, we're talking like a bunch of high schoolers. We're supposed to be mature teachers, remember? Not a couple of little crush cadets. They arrive on Tuesday."

Teri laughed aloud, and several of the teachers cast a glance her direction to see what was so funny. "That was very good, Jessica! I'm going to remember that: 'little crush cadets.' I like that."

Jessica had to smile. She hadn't even realized that's what she had said. Attempting to persuade Teri of her seriousness, Jessica said in a hushed voice, "Nothing is going on between Kyle and me, okay?"

Teri stopped laughing, but her smirk remained. "You know, Jessica, denial is a wonderful thing when you're in pain. It's *not* such a wonderful thing when you're in love."

"Pain?" Jessica questioned. She had learned a bit about pain lately. "Love?" she asked, secretly knowing that she knew very little about love. Then almost under her breath she said to Teri, "Aren't they both about the same thing?"

Teri looked at Jessica, her expression turning more solemn. "I don't suppose they have to be, but sometimes I suppose they are."

Ms. Mendelson strode back to her podium and called the meeting to order. Jessica didn't turn around to check if Kyle were still at his post at the door. It bothered her that she still felt fluttery in her stomach and decided the abundance of potato salad must be the cause. It certainly couldn't be her emotions. If she couldn't control those at age twenty-five, well then she might as well be a—what had she called them? Little crush cadets. Of course, Jessica *Fenton* could not risk anyone or anything controlling her, especially her own unruly emotions.

The meeting broke at nearly five o'clock. Jessica felt exhausted; she was eager to get home and collapse on the couch. But at the last minute she decided to return to her classroom for one of the textbooks she hadn't finished looking over. When she opened the door, Kyle was standing on a ladder checking something in the ceiling.

"Hi," he said warmly as Jessica entered the room.

"Hi. Everything okay up there?" She checked her tone of voice, expression, and body language, being careful to address Kyle as she would any random firefighter who might be lurking in her room.

"Yep. The sprinkler system checks out fine. So this is your room, huh?" he asked, coming down the ladder. Jessica wondered if he already knew that and had been waiting for her to return.

"Yes, this is my room."

"Looks as if you're all ready for the big day."

"I need to look through one more of the textbooks," she said, reaching for the book on the shelf behind Kyle. Why did she feel she had to explain to him her reason for being in her own room?

"So you're going to be pretty busy tonight reading your textbook?" Kyle asked.

Jessica wasn't sure what to say. She held the book to her chest, with her arms crossed, and looked down at her shoes. She knew what Kyle was going to ask her next, and she didn't want to answer him until the blush had faded from her cheeks.

Just then the door to her room opened. "Hey, Jess," Teri called out, "do you want a ride—" She stopped mid-sentence. "Oh hi, Kyle."

Jessica turned to face Teri and tried to appear natural. She guessed the blushing hadn't completely faded yet, because Teri raised her eyebrows and said, "I guess Kyle can give you a ride

home. If that wouldn't be too much of a *pain* for you, Kyle."
Jessica caught the hidden meaning of Teri's emphasis on "pain."

"Sure," Kyle obliged quickly. "I'd be glad to."

Jessica shot Teri a look that said, "What are you doing to me?"

Teri only smiled back, nodded, and said, "Okay, so I'll see you tomorrow, Jess. And I'll see you whenever, Kyle. Bye, you guys." With that, she disappeared.

"Did you need to get anything else?" Kyle asked as he folded up the ladder.

"No, this is it." She walked back to the door with Kyle behind her, toting the ladder with one hand. Jessica gathered up her purse, handbook, and notes from the day, along with Teri's aloe vera plant.

"Can I carry anything for you?" Kyle offered.

"No, I have it all. Thanks."

They walked silently down the hallway. Several other teachers greeted them, calling Kyle by name and nodding at Jessica as if they recognized her but didn't quite remember her name. She wondered if it looked as if she and Kyle were "together," and she wished they would pass Martin Monroe. She would love to give Martin the impression she wasn't available.

Kyle returned the ladder to a storage closet near the front door, and they exited together. Jessica adjusted the awkward cargo in her arms and started down the front steps. On the fourth cement step, her left leg wobbled, and she nearly fell. Kyle reached for her elbow and gently held on to her, steadying her steps the rest of the way.

"You sure I can't hold that plant for you?" he asked.

"Thanks, but I have it," Jessica said stubbornly. Kyle released her elbow.

They were almost to his white truck in the parking lot

when Charlotte came sprinting up behind them, her spike heels clicking on the asphalt. She must have spotted them leaving from her office window. Maybe she saw Kyle holding Jessica's elbow.

"Kyle, you didn't check out at my office." She caught up with them and positioned herself between Jessica and Kyle, with her back to Jessica. Charlotte said sharply, "You must come back to the office so I can sign the papers."

Jessica couldn't help but cough when the overwhelming scent of Charlotte's perfume met her nostrils. Either she had just doused herself, or the jog to the parking lot had activated the fragrance at her pulse points.

Kyle explained that he had returned the papers to the office already and that Mrs. Blair, the secretary, had put them in Charlotte's office. As Charlotte continued to try to persuade Kyle to come back with her and show her where they were, Jessica realized that Kyle had, indeed, already completed his inspection and was waiting for her in her room. Teri might actually be right. Maybe Kyle was interested in her in more than a benevolent way.

Jessica wanted to feel flattered, but she couldn't allow herself the luxury. Instead, she thought she should run away, leave Charlotte and Kyle in the parking lot, and walk home, ignoring both of them and refusing to deal with the emotions either of them evoked in her. She would watch for her little squirrel friends and think up stories and feel nothing for real people. That was the only safe place for her to be.

Before she had a chance to act on her impulse, Kyle stepped around Charlotte and gently took Jessica again by the arm. He said, "I'm sure you'll find the papers on your desk. If not, Mrs. Blair can direct you to them."

"But we haven't discussed the assembly," Charlotte said, following them to the truck.

"I arranged it with Mrs. Blair. Twenty-minute talk at 9:30 on Tuesday, September 28. It's a standard career presentation." Kyle unlocked the passenger door and assisted Jessica into the cab. He closed the door and walked around to his door. Charlotte followed him. Kyle politely said, "Good day," got into the cab, and started the engine.

Charlotte Mendelson's gaze left Kyle, and she caught Jessica's glance. She shot Jessica a venomous expression. For an instant, Jessica felt her hair bristle, but then she forced herself to look away, breaking the poisonous spell. That woman would *not* control her.

Kyle drove slowly out of the parking lot, opening the glove compartment, taking out a pack of cinnamon flavored gum, and offering Jessica a stick.

"No thanks."

Kyle unwrapped his piece while holding the steering wheel with his thigh. Soon the cab filled with the faint scent of cinnamon. Jessica remembered when Kyle had leaned into her car and instructed her to breathe slowly. The cinnamon scent on his breath had comforted her then, and it soothed her now.

Kyle turned down Marigold Lane and then ventured to ask Jessica, "Are you going to be busy tonight, then?"

"I really do have a lot I need to do." Jessica was beginning to dislike herself and the aloof role she was playing. *Whatever you do, Jess, don't look at him. If Charlotte's look can make your skin crawl, Kyle's could certainly make your heart melt. Don't let it!*

Chapter Seven

*K*yle pulled up in front of Jessica's little cottage and
turned off the truck's engine.

"Thanks for the ride," Jessica said, trying to let him know
she appreciated his kindness, even though she couldn't return
his interest in her. Jessica opened the truck's door, collected her
things, and began to step out. Her left leg gave way as she
placed her weight on it. Reaching for the door to steady herself, she clutched the plant while half her loose papers fluttered
to the ground.

Kyle sprang from his side of the vehicle and dashed around
to help Jessica regain her balance. "I'm okay," she said, refusing
his helping hand. "My leg still stiffens up. It must be from sitting all day."

"Let me carry these for you," Kyle said, gathering the papers
before the wind had a chance to scatter them. Jessica thought it
would be ridiculous to refuse his assistance for such a small
thing. She made it to the front door without further mishaps.

As they walked inside, the smell of last night's burnt zucchini greeted them. She hoped Kyle wouldn't notice. But then, he was a firefighter.

"Did something get burned in the kitchen recently?" Kyle asked, sniffing the air like Smoky the Bear.

"It was only some zucchini I overcooked last night. Nothing, really." Jessica hoped he would leave it at that.

"Do you have a smoke detector in there?" Kyle wandered into the kitchen.

"Yes," Jessica said, following him. She pointed to the round ivory device above the refrigerator, but didn't mention it had gone off last night.

"By any chance did Ida have a safety check done on this place before you moved in?" Kyle asked. "I could do one for you real quick, if you don't mind."

How could she refuse a safety check?

Kyle began by looking under the sink and following the electrical plug in from the coffeemaker and toaster oven to the wall outlet. He effortlessly pulled out the refrigerator, checked behind it, rolled it back, and then opened the refrigerator door.

Jessica held her breath. Would he notice it was empty? Of course he would.

Kyle stood still a moment, the door open, studying the dial in the back of the cold box. "Everything looks good," he said, closing the door but not asking why it was empty. "Nice and safe."

That's how Jessica was beginning to involuntarily feel around Kyle, nice and safe. But she couldn't, she wouldn't. She wasn't supposed to meet someone like Kyle in Glenbrooke. Something drastic needed to be done, and it needed to be done *now*.

"Look, Kyle," Jessica said, "I appreciate all the nice things you've done for me. Thank you. But you have to leave me alone. I can't have you waiting for me in my classroom or carrying my books home from school or checking my kitchen for fire hazards." Her voice was rising to a near shouting level. "I'm sorry I have to say this to you, but please leave me alone."

It took everything within her to hold back the tears. "I mean it. Leave me alone! Just leave me alone!" She was yelling now as she pointed to the door.

Kyle looked stunned. He stood his ground and said, "What is it, Jessica? What's the problem?"

Jessica had to look away from him. The instant she did, the tears began to overflow and came crashing down her fiery red cheeks. Depleted of her burst of anger, Jessica spoke mechanically and repeated her request in a lower tone. "Just leave me alone."

"Not until you tell me why."

"I can't."

"Is it another guy? Financial problems? What is it, Jessica? I can help, if you'd let me."

Jessica blinked hard and tried to find another compartment of anger inside herself from which to draw her response. "It's none of your business," she said levelly. "Leave me alone."

She turned her back on Kyle and limped through the kitchen and out her back door so she could be the one to slam a door behind her. Collapsing into the chaise lounge, Jessica let the tears fall—tears for how she had just treated Kyle, tears for the pain creeping up her leg, tears for all the fears she was running away from.

The back door opened, and slow, deliberate footsteps approached her. Jessica refused to look at Kyle. She commanded her tears to halt, but they refused to obey. Kyle stopped behind her. She wouldn't turn around.

"Jessica, let me tell you something about secrets." His words were firm and delivered with what sounded like deep rage. "The longer you carry them, the heavier they become." With that, he turned and marched away. This time, it was Kyle's turn to slam the door.

What is that supposed to mean? What does he know about my secrets?

Jessica rose and angrily walked to the front door. The minute she reached it, she could hear the engine of Kyle's truck rumble to a roar and the tires squeal as they peeled away from the curb.

She stood there for a long time. Finally her throbbing leg persuaded her to climb the stairs and soak in a long, hot bath. While she sat in the tub, Jessica tried to convince herself she had done the right thing.

On Friday, she sat uncomfortably through the morning session of endless and, in her opinion, unnecessary meetings led by their commander in chief. Teri wisely didn't bring up the subject of Kyle. The meetings ended at noon so there was no catered buffet. Jessica hoped the donut and orange juice she had gleaned from the snack table that morning would hold her through the rest of the day. She had finished the remainder of her sandwich, which she had smuggled into her purse at yesterday's lunch, and she had nothing at home.

When the teachers were dismissed, Charlotte announced over the microphone, "I need to see Ms. Fenton immediately in my office."

"Do you want me to go with you?" Teri asked. "I can come in looking for a requisition form or something."

"No, Charlotte doesn't scare me. Look, she's up there talking to that P.E. coach again. I think I'll go on over and be waiting for her in her office."

"You do that," Teri said. "Hey, are we still on for tonight? I have cheerleading practice with the girls until 5:30. I could come pick you up after that."

"I didn't know you were in charge of the cheerleaders."

"Yeah, sort of a flashback to my old days at Kelley High School in Escondido. I was a cheerleader my senior year. I almost didn't make it, but…" Teri and Jessica both noticed Charlotte leaving the podium and making her way out the front door toward her office. "Well, that's a story for another day."

"Go ahead and tell me now. Charlotte can wait."

"No, it's kind of a long story. I'll pick you up after 5:30, okay?"

"Okay," Jessica agreed. Teri went her way, leaving Jessica to make the journey to the office alone.

Charlotte wasn't there when Jessica arrived so she went in, at the secretary's recommendation, and took a seat facing the wide desk and full bookshelves. One of the books caught Jessica's eye. She wanted a closer look. Checking over her shoulder to make sure Charlotte wasn't about to walk through the open door, Jessica slid over to the bookshelf and pulled out the book.

It was old, like the antique books that filled her own shelf. Jessica carefully opened the book and read the copyright, "London, Chapman and Hall, 1872." The binding on the book next to it read, "Essays, First Series, Emerson." Jessica paused. It was a book of essays by Ralph Waldo Emerson, a book she would be thrilled to add to her collection. She carefully put the book back and scanned the spines of the others on the shelf. The collection was impressive, and it belonged to Charlotte Mendelson.

Jessica returned to her seat perplexed. She never would have guessed that Charlotte had a love for classical literature. It had been easy to write off Charlotte when she seemed to have no human side to her. Now Jessica found it difficult and painful to continue disliking a person who shared her hobby.

It also seemed a pity that she would never be able to compare collections and swap stories of how the treasured volumes were acquired.

The office door swung open, and Charlotte marched in. "We seem to have a problem with your files, Ms. Fenton. You failed to list anything under 'nearest relative'."

From the look in Charlotte's eyes, Jessica knew she was out for blood. All thoughts of common interests evaporated.

"We need a name, address, and phone number in case of emergency."

"Okay, I'll bring it in on Tuesday," Jessica said coolly.

"You mean you don't know your parents' name, address, and phone number?" Charlotte mocked.

Jessica paused before answering. "My mother is dead. Now if you'll excuse me," she rose from her chair, "I'll bring the information in for you on Tuesday, like I said." Jessica began to walk stiffly to the door.

As Jessica reached for the knob, she heard Charlotte say in a low voice, "I see it left a scar. Too bad." Her voice displayed no pity.

Jessica's hand froze on the knob. It took everything within her to ignore the comment and continue out the door. She succeeded. She even closed the door calmly and said hello to Mrs. Blair, the secretary. Mrs. Blair looked as if she had aged five years since Jessica had seen her on Monday. The phone was ringing, papers were everywhere, and the woman had spilled coffee or hot chocolate down the front of her white blouse. Jessica wondered how long Mrs. Blair would last in her position. Having Mr. McGregor as principal must have been quite different.

Jessica walked home slowly, forcing all thoughts of Charlotte to flee. It was a warm afternoon, and she enjoyed the old homes in her neighborhood. Each house was different.

Some of the houses had broad porches and inviting porch swings. Other homes looked colonial with white, fat columns out front, boasting that someone important lived there. Next to one such mansion was wedged a little white bungalow with green flower boxes in the front. Eighty years ago, the servants to the big house probably lived there. Or maybe it used to be the carriage house. Today, it was someone's starter home and probably cost more than the servants who used to live there had made in their entire lifetimes.

The hot afternoon sun made it seem as if it were the middle of summer, with many more weeks of warm nights, watermelons, and giggling children running through sprinklers. Only the sunflowers at the house on the corner of Marigold Lane gave away the truth. Their five-foot-tall stalks sagged. All of them had popped their seeds and seemed to beg for a chance to lie down in the compost pile. A few more golden days and then the cool winds would come, and with the winds, the rain.

Everything in Glenbrooke was the way Jessica had thought it would be, as far as the houses, weather, and neighbors were concerned. She stopped on the sidewalk two doors away from her cottage and watched something she never saw in Los Angeles: white sheets flapping in the wind on a clothesline. A woman about her age clipped the last fresh, white pillowcase on the line while a tow-headed toddler waddled around the clothesline pole, contentedly singing to himself. The scene made Jessica's heart ache. She wanted to be the woman hanging clothes on the line. She wanted a little blond boy to sing at her feet.

Striding to her home, Jessica unlocked the door, went straight upstairs to her room, and opened the barrel top of the old trunk at the foot of her bed. Underneath her black felt hat and a box of Italian leather gloves, Jessica pulled out the photo album she had brought with her.

Before she opened it, she decided the occasion was worth using her last tea bag. She brewed herself a cup of tea, good and strong, and then retreated back to her bedroom where the album awaited her.

The afternoon sun pierced through the fluttering lace curtains, tracing its warm pattern of light on the floor. Jessica sat in the middle of the mosaic, with her back pressed against the old trunk. Slowly, she opened the family photo album. Having looked at it a thousand times, she had each page memorized. When she got to the fourth page, she stopped. There, in the upper right-hand corner, was the picture she was looking for. It was a black and white snapshot nearly identical to the scene she had just viewed. A curly haired, aproned woman with wooden clothespins in her mouth was hanging white sheets on a line. At her feet stood a grinning little girl in pigtails, proudly handing her mama a pillowcase from the wicker basket full of clean clothes. The little girl posed for the camera. Short little dress. Left sock scrunched down around her black shoe. She was endearing. And she was Jessica's mother.

Releasing a heartbroken sigh, Jessica mourned the loss of her mother as the dust fairies rode in the beams of sunlight and floated around her. They were her only consolers this afternoon.

No one had ever mourned with Jessica. Not even that first day when she came home from school. She was eight, about the same age as her mother had been in that photo. Jessica had walked into the house, and Aunt Bonnie had grasped her by the hand and ushered her into the kitchen for some milk and cookies.

"Why are you here, Aunt Bonnie?" Jessica had asked. "Did Uncle John come too?"

"No, Jessie. I'm here because your mommy was sick."

"She only got sick two days ago. She'll be better soon."

"Well, Jessie, sometimes people don't get better. Sometimes they have to go somewhere else."

"You mean to the hospital?"

"No, I don't mean to the hospital, Jessie. Sometimes people have to leave us. You see, your mommy is gone. She went to be an angel."

Jessica remembered how her Aunt Bonnie had begun to cry and how Jessica hadn't understood, so she was the one who comforted Aunt Bonnie without shedding a tear of her own. And she didn't cry later. Not when her dad came home that night from his business trip and wrapped her in his arms and cried until the top of her pink mouse pajamas was soaked. Not when she sat on the deck of a sleek yacht off the coast of Catalina Island and watched the grown-ups cry as they sprinkled some white powder in the water.

She hadn't cried. Until now. At twenty-five and all alone, Jessica finally cried, hugging her knees and rocking herself back and forth, back and forth. First she sobbed silently, then audibly, then from deep within the core of her. She groaned and mourned until she finally surrendered to her grief.

Exhausted, she lay on the floor. Then sleep came to Jessica, sweet, soothing sleep with the end of the summer sun as her blanket.

Somewhere in her foggy dream, Jessica heard a voice calling her name and then loud knocking. Shaking herself awake, she realized someone was downstairs knocking on her door.

Teri.

"I'll be right there!" she called out and tried to pull herself together. Carefully nudging her stiff legs down the stairs, Jessica opened the front door and began to apologize. "I fell asleep. I'm not feeling really great, Teri. Would it be okay if I took a rain check on tonight?"

Teri carefully looked at her and asked, "Are you sure you're okay? Is there anything I can do?"

"I think I need to sleep, that's all."

"Should I come in and fix you something to eat? Some soup or something?"

"No," Jessica said, responding a little too quickly. "I mean, no thanks. I'm not hungry. I'll be fine. I'm sorry I didn't call you, and you had to drive all the way over here."

"All the way over?" Teri said. "It's half a mile, and you're on my way home anyway." Teri took one last look. "You sure you're okay?"

Jessica forced the most convincing grin she could find. "It's been a full week."

"I'll call you tomorrow," Teri promised.

"Okay. Fine. Bye." Jessica gave a weak wave, closed and bolted the door, and returned upstairs. She opened her dresser drawer, looking for some clean pajamas. The first thing she grabbed turned out to be a large T-shirt, which she slipped into and crawled into bed. Her arm brushed across the front of the shirt. It felt rough. Then she realized it was the letters on the T-shirt, the ones that spelled out, "Eleventh Annual Glenbrooke Firefighters' Pancake Breakfast." Kyle's shirt.

Jessica refused to be moved. Part of her wanted to surrender her stubborn will and devise a way to be reconciled with Kyle. Another part of her wanted to push Kyle far away so she could carry out her plan without having his feelings—and hers—get in the way. She had to keep pushing away everything and everyone who tried to soften her, who would lower her defenses. It was just a stupid old T-shirt. It meant nothing.

She lay for a long time, staring at the wall while the sun went down, slowly extinguishing all natural light in her room. Somewhere down the street she could hear the shouts and squeals of children on roller blades playing one last round of street hockey.

Autumn was coming. She could smell it in the evening breeze. At the base of the rose trellis out by her front door, a lonely cricket chirped. Jessica knew his song. She knew he would stay there all night. *Go ahead, little buddy. Sing your heart out. I'm not letting you inside.*

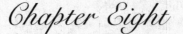

Chapter Eight

*H*ello? Yes, I'd like Hugh McGregor's room, please," Jessica said to the hospital operator.

"Hello, this is Ida."

"Hi, Ida. It's Jessica."

"Oh, Jessica, dear. I should have called you and invited you to the hospital with me. I thought with it being Saturday and all that you would have a busy day planned. You call me next time you want to come, okay?"

Jessica was beginning to hate being without transportation and so dependent on others. "How is Mr. McGregor doing?"

"Wonderful, dear. Just wonderful! He's regained eighty percent of his movement or whatever they call it, and he goes home on Tuesday. Isn't that wonderful news? He's right here. Why don't you tell him hello?"

Jessica spoke with Hugh McGregor for a few minutes, and he really did sound better. She gingerly asked about her file, which he had mentioned when she visited him.

"It's not complete," Hugh said.

Jessica already knew that. Was he trying to tell her something more, but couldn't because Ida was there? Jessica told him to rest, and she promised to call on Sunday. Ida got back on the phone and reminded Jessica of the times of the two church services on Sunday and the picnic on Monday. Jessica thanked her, but knew she wouldn't go to either.

She planned to stay home, all by herself, the entire weekend. She had made the decision last night after Teri came by. Being around other people felt too difficult right now when she felt so emotional. It would be better and safer to be alone.

But the biggest problem with being alone was that she spent too many hours thinking of all the things that could go wrong in her life and all the things that already had. Kyle was definitely on the list. Jessica knew she would see him again, this being a small town and all. What would she say?

The only time she ventured out of the house all weekend was late Saturday afternoon. A corner market was located about five blocks away, and Jessica was desperate for food. She hadn't eaten anything since the donut and orange juice at school on Friday morning. With a meager $10.27 in her purse, she hiked to the little market and came home with a full bag of groceries. She ate a slice of day-old bread as she walked. The loaf had cost only thirty-nine cents. Jessica decided if she tried really hard, the eggs, bread, canned beans, and fruit might last her the entire week.

Best of all, Jessica realized for the first time that Oregon had no sales tax. That meant she had received change, leaving her with eighty-four cents in the bottom of her purse.

The absurdity of her situation made her laugh. Never would she have guessed that she would be walking down the street in Oregon with only eighty-four cents to her name. The laughing part she would have guessed, though. She had known she would be happy here. She had always known she was a small-town girl at heart, just like her mom had been.

When Jessica was halfway home, she noticed a white truck that looked like Kyle's parked at the end of the next block. Part of her wanted to run the other way and part of her wanted to face him and get it over. Without completely making up her mind, Jessica walked toward the truck.

It might not even be his. If it is and he sees me and asks what I'm doing on this block, I can always say I got lost. And if he sees me with a bag of groceries, that would be good. He would think I simply hadn't been to the store yet, and that's why my refrigerator was empty when he came over.

Before she knew it, Jessica was standing a few feet away from the truck. It was Kyle's all right. She wondered which house he was in. That's when she noticed the cemetery across the street. Kyle was bending down on one knee, placing a bouquet of daisies in front of one of the graves. Jessica wanted to watch. She thought of hiding behind a tree and then going over to see the name on the grave. But it would never work. She couldn't hide, because there weren't any trees on her side of the street. The huge trees were all at the cemetery, and if she tried to sneak to the other side of the street to try to hide behind a tree—with her bag of groceries in tow—he would surely see her. Besides, it seemed inappropriate to spy on someone in such a private moment.

Jessica turned around and walked swiftly back the way she came. *What if he gets in his truck, drives this way, and sees me?*

By the time she reached her front door, she was panting from her rapid pace. Quickly turning the key in the lock, Jessica slipped inside, closed the door, and let out a huge sigh. It was ridiculous to act so juvenile. Why did she push this man away, then two days later stalk him, only to run away again? How could she possibly trust herself to make rational decisions the next time she saw him?

Jessica put away her treasured, if scant, groceries and thought about old love songs that mentioned doing crazy things when you're in love. Jessica wondered if her personal life were different now. If she were in Glenbrooke under different circumstances, would she allow herself to fall in love with Kyle?

"It's ridiculous," Jessica scolded herself aloud as she filled a pan with water and prepared to boil an egg for her dinner. "I don't know a thing about him. How can you fall in love with a stranger?"

Jessica dined on her boiled egg and a glass of water, eating in front of the TV, changing channels until she came on an old black-and-white movie that was just starting. She had seen this one before but was glad she couldn't remember how it ended.

That's how Jessica spent the rest of the weekend, eating only when necessary, relaxing with her antique book collection, and watching old movies on TV. The food commercials were her only frustration. She quickly switched the channel every time another tantalizing ad came on, and she promised herself a freezer full of DoveBars when her paycheck came.

By Tuesday morning, she felt rested, calm, and ready for the challenge that lay ahead of her. It was a good thing, because the next four days were nonstop.

After all the talk Jessica had heard about Dawn, she was surprised to find her to be an ordinary high school student. Dawn's long, straight blond hair hung down her back, and her round face looked innocent. Jessica felt drawn to her.

During the first few days of school, she looked for an opportunity to talk with Dawn, not that she was sure what she would say. The chance came on Wednesday after class. Dawn came up to Jessica's desk while the rest of the class scattered into the hallway.

"I was wondering if you would like to buy a candy bar. It's to raise money for an outreach trip to Mexico," Dawn said.

Jessica wished she could feel freer with her money. "I'm sorry, Dawn. Not this time. Try me after payday."

"Okay," Dawn said and was about to leave when Jessica stopped her.

"Dawn?"

"Yes?" She looked so young when she turned and met Jessica's gaze.

"I want you to know that my door is always open to you, if you have any questions about class or whatever. Sorry I couldn't help out with the fund-raiser this week."

"That's okay. See you tomorrow."

Jessica nodded and watched Dawn hurry out the door. The classroom had begun to fill with next period's students. Jessica watched them slide into their seats and chat with each other. They were great students. She liked all of them. But she felt something stronger toward Dawn, in the same way she was more drawn to Teri than to any of the other teachers she had met.

Teri seemed to feel the same way about Jessica, because she continued to seek out Jessica during the week. On Friday afternoon Teri sat on the edge of Jessica's desk and said, "So you think you're ready to come back next Monday and do this all over again?"

"What a first week!" Jessica shook her head. "I can't believe it went so fast."

Teri slowly rotated her head in small circles, trying to relax. "And just think—that was only four days. Next week we get to do this for five! And the next week, and the next week…" Her voice faded as she continued the small circles.

She looked like a teacher in her navy blue, straight jumper and white shirt. Jessica noticed that Teri never wore jewelry, and yet somehow her outfits always looked complete and stylishly put together.

In contrast, Jessica had accessories to go with every outfit she owned. Today she wore a DKNY brown knit skirt and matching sweater. It turned out to be a warmer day than she had thought, and she had pushed up the sleeves so many times that now the sweater felt all itchy in the crook of her elbow.

"Do you have another chiropractor appointment today?" Teri asked.

"No, I went yesterday. Ida took me. I can't imagine what kind of shape I'd be in if I hadn't started going to Dr. Dane right after the accident. Have you ever had one of Becky's massages?"

"No, but it sounds pretty wonderful right about now," Teri said. "What are you going to do this weekend?"

"Nothing much. Work on lesson plans maybe," Jessica said.

"Do you want to come over tonight for leftover spaghetti? I know you weren't up for doing anything last Friday night, and if you aren't this week either, I'll understand."

Jessica thought of how she was down to her last two eggs and four pieces of bread. She had managed to hoard that final eighty-four cents, though! Payday was still a week away. A free meal would be wonderful, and it would be nice to spend the evening with Teri.

"Sure. Spaghetti sounds great. Do you want me to bring anything?" Jessica wasn't sure why she asked; she couldn't bring anything even if Teri asked her to. Fortunately Teri said she had a full refrigerator.

They stopped by Jessica's long enough for her to change into jeans, and then they drove the six or so blocks to Teri's little house. It was an old house like Jessica's, but not quite as charming. Perhaps the bungalow's color took away from its appeal—mint green with ivory trim.

The one-story rental house had two bedrooms and a full basement. Inside, everything was cream and white and simple. The kitchen table had white chairs and was covered with an ivory tablecloth. A basket of linen napkins sat in the center of the table with tall white salt and pepper shakers on either side. Teri took Jessica on a quick tour of her comfortable, light and airy home, which concluded once again in the kitchen where Teri started to fix dinner.

While she worked, she told stories about where she had picked up most of the furniture. She bought her plants at moving sales, which she watched for in the paper, and her dishes were a collection of old china plates she had picked up at a variety of garage sales. She handed Jessica a china plate that had rich blue and yellow flowers etched around the edge and invited her to help herself to the tossed salad in the big wooden bowl on the counter.

Even though Teri and Jessica saw each other at school every day and had chatted some here and there, they really hadn't talked with each other in depth. Jessica felt comfortable with the casualness of their friendship and was thankful Teri hadn't done any probing. As long as that was how their conversations stayed, they would be fine.

"Did you see Mr. McGregor yesterday?" Teri asked.

Jessica poured some Thousand Island dressing on her salad and said, "Yes. He's home now, and he seems to be doing lots better. The home nurse who looks after him is a real sweetie. I don't think he'll be back at school for some time, though. I'm afraid we're stuck with Charlotte the rest of the year."

Teri scooped some spaghetti noodles onto her plate and held another helping in midair, waiting for Jessica's plate. "Did you sign that card Charlotte bought for Mr. McGregor? She made him a blueberry cheesecake and took it over yesterday."

Jessica still couldn't imagine Charlotte as anything other than villain. Why would she buy a card and make a cheese-cake? She had to have something to gain. "No, I didn't know a card was going around."

"Kyle was over there when she showed up, and he said the cheesecake could win first place at the county fair. Say, Jessica, whatever happened with you and Kyle? I thought something was about to start up between you two, but you haven't said a word about him, and he hasn't been around."

"I guess nothing is happening," Jessica said, ladling the hot marinara sauce over her noodles and then sitting down at the kitchen table.

"He asked about you at the Labor Day picnic on Monday," Teri said.

"Your church picnic?" Jessica asked.

"Yes, Kyle goes to my church," Teri said, joining Jessica at the table. "He works with the teenagers. A sort of volunteer youth pastor."

Kyle goes to church and works with teens. I suppose I should have guessed. Everyone in this town goes to church. Jessica was about to question Teri as to what Kyle had said, but Teri spoke first.

"Do you mind if I say grace?"

Jessica shrugged her shoulders. "Go ahead."

Teri prayed, and Jessica half lowered her eyes and looked at the cucumber slice in her salad. It was more out of respect for Teri than for God. How could Teri talk aloud to God so nat-urally? It was peculiar, but nice, in a small-town sort of way.

They started to eat, and Jessica hoped the subject would change, but Teri brought it back to Kyle. "He's taking a group of kids from church down to Mexico next month. Didn't any of them try to sell you a candy bar this week? They've been working to raise the money ever since their trip last year."

"As a matter of fact, Dawn Laughlin asked me if I wanted to buy a candy bar. Is she actually going to Mexico?"

"Yes, she is," Teri said, cutting her spaghetti before eating it. "I think it will be the best thing in the world for her. She knows all about wealth and fancy hotels in Paris; it's time she learned how others live. Besides, I'm the one who talked her into going."

"You must be a good persuader," Jessica said. "Mexico is not for everyone."

Teri's brown eyes grew wide, she put down her fork and looked at Jessica. "Why don't you go too?" she asked enthusiastically. "It's such a great trip. You'll love it!"

"Me? Go to Mexico? I don't think so, Teri. I'm not very interested in that sort of thing."

"Oh, come on! I'm going. I went last year, too. I'm their official interpreter. Do you speak any Spanish?"

"Tacos," Jessica said, her mouth full of salad. "And huevos rancheros." She swallowed her bite. "That's about it. Not quite enough to qualify as an interpreter."

"What we need," Teri said with a rather determined gleam in her eye, "is another adult chaperone. It's only Kyle and me at this point, and we have at least twelve and maybe fourteen kids going."

Jessica shook her head. She would never go to a place like Mexico to chaperone a bunch of kids, especially for a church outing. Especially when Kyle was going. "No, Teri, really. You'd be better off finding someone else."

"Like who? Martin the Masher? Ms. Mendelson?"

Jessica kept on eating. She would not be persuaded.

"Take a week to think about it. I'll ask you again," Teri said, the determined lines on her forehead easing away. "We don't leave for three weeks."

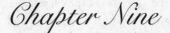

Chapter Nine

*T*rue to her word, Teri showed up in Jessica's classroom a week later on Friday afternoon and said, "Well?"

"Well, what?"

"I've given you a week to think about it. Have you changed your mind about Mexico?"

"Mexico?" Jessica had thought of many things that week, but Mexico was not on the list. "If you mean will I go with your church group, I don't think so, Teri. You can tell me all about it when you come back. I'll even watch up to three hours of slides."

Teri laughed. "With free popcorn, right?"

Jessica smiled back. The thought of popcorn made her mouth water. Her food situation had gone from bad to worse. Each day she had made trips to the teachers' lounge where a box of donuts, some muffins, or banana bread usually sat out on the table. If another teacher was in the room, she would take only a small portion. If the room was empty, she would eagerly reach for the free food and eat each morsel.

With her final eighty-four cents she had bought another loaf of day-old bread and two packages of Ramen noodles on Wednesday. She really disliked Ramen noodles, but they were the cheapest item in the store. Her purchase that day had actually come to eighty-nine cents, and she had sheepishly apologized to the clerk that she didn't have the additional nickel. A little boy behind her handed Jessica a nickel and said, "I got fifteen nickels for all my pop cans. You want one?" Jessica thanked the boy, wrote down his name, and promised to pay him back.

Today was payday. She was saved. She could go to the bank, open an account with her check, keep some of the money, and begin to live a normal life.

But each of the four times she had checked her box today, it had been empty. She could see the white paycheck envelopes in all the other teachers' boxes, but none was in hers.

"Would you like a ride home?" Teri asked.

"I need to check on something in the office," Jessica said. "Maybe you better go on. I don't want to hold you up since I know you have to be at the game early tonight with your cheerleader squad."

"I have time. I can wait."

"No, really," Jessica said. "You go on. I don't know how long I'll be here."

"Okay. Call me if you want a ride to the game tonight."

"I will. Thanks."

Jessica felt relieved to be on her own. Teri had given her a ride nearly every night, and on Wednesday, Ida had picked her up so she could go to the chiropractor and visit Mr. McGregor. When Ida left the room to find a vase for the flowers she had brought, Jessica had asked him again about her file. All he said was, "It's not complete."

"I know," Jessica replied. "Charlotte has already talked with me about it. I'm sure it will be fine. Don't worry."

Hugh had shaken his head slowly. "I don't feel good about this."

"About what?"

"About you coming to Glenbrooke to hide. None of us can ever really hide, Jessica. The truth has a way of surfacing when we least expect it."

Jessica had patted Mr. McGregor's hand and said, "Don't worry about me. I'm fine." And she had really believed she was.

After all, she had a home, she was enjoying teaching, and today she would get paid.

After Teri left, Jessica closed up her classroom and headed for the office, practicing how she would ask for her check. She had never asked for money before in her life. If Mrs. Blair wasn't in the office, she would have to discuss the matter with Charlotte.

As long as she had kept her distance from Charlotte these past two weeks, everything had been fine. But then, Kyle hadn't been around, and that made it hard to define everything as "fine." Jessica hadn't seen him since that afternoon at the cemetery. It was horrible waiting to bump into him. She watched each white truck that went by on her walk to school, and every time she heard the faint whine of a fire-truck siren in the middle of class, she involuntarily wondered if Kyle might be the driver. Was he going to rescue someone else? Had he already?

Jessica stepped into the school office and shook away her haphazard thoughts. Mrs. Blair sat at her desk, nearly in tears.

"Are you okay?" Jessica asked.

Mrs. Blair looked up, startled. "Yes, yes, of course. What can I do for you, Jessica?"

"I didn't find my paycheck in my box, and I wondered if you knew anything about it."

The intercom buzzed on Mrs. Blair's disheveled desk. Both she and Jessica jumped.

"Tell Ms. Fenton I'll see her in my office."

Jessica and Mrs. Blair exchanged glances. Jessica drew up her shoulders, sucked in a deep breath, and said, "You have a good weekend, Mrs. Blair." She walked into Charlotte's office like a woman who was afraid of nothing and no one.

"Were you wondering about your check, Ms. Fenton?"

"Today is payday, right?" Jessica answered with a question, refusing to let Charlotte have the upper hand.

"You failed to provide the information I requested." Charlotte held in front of Jessica a form with Jessica's name at the top and pointed with a red acrylic nail at the blank line under "nearest relative."

Jessica remembered that she had said she would bring in a number on the first day of school, but she had completely forgotten. She felt like a student being reprimanded for forgetting her homework; she vowed never to make one of her students feel the way she felt right now.

"I can bring in that number on Monday. It's not a problem."

"Oh, yes, it is a problem. You see, I've called the district office, and they don't seem to have a copy of your file anywhere. They don't seem to think that you exist. Teachers who don't exist don't receive paychecks."

"Then let's call Hugh and have him talk to the district office," Jessica said, trying to keep the tone of her voice on an even keel and not reveal any of the frantic emotions that had just broken forth inside of her. She had a horrible realization that Mr. McGregor must have registered her as Jessica Morgan, since the fake last name of Fenton came after she arrived in Glenbrooke. She also realized that she didn't have any ID. How would she ever cash her check or open a bank account? After all the things she had worried about and lain awake at night thinking about, why hadn't these obvious facts occurred to her?

"I've already called Hugh," Charlotte said crisply. "I asked him when he sent in the file for Jessica Fenton, and do you know what he told me?"

Jessica could feel her temperature rising and her cheeks beginning to burn. She forced herself to show no emotion.

"He said he didn't know anyone named Jessica Fenton, and did I mean Jessica Morgan."

A fiery arrow of fear shot through Jessica. Why, oh, why hadn't she warned Mr. McGregor, or at least told him she was going by the name Fenton? Jessica tried to think quickly. "It's really not that complicated. Morgan was my step-father's name," Jessica lied, "and I chose to go back to my birth name when my mother died. Slight mix-up, that's all. I'd like my file at the district office changed to Fenton."

"I've asked for your file to be sent directly to me," Charlotte said, her expression not revealing if she believed Jessica's lie or not. "We'll see about changing it once it arrives."

"In the meantime," Jessica said, directing some of her pent up emotions into anger, "what am I supposed to do for a paycheck?"

"Wait," Charlotte said, leaning back in her chair.

"You can't do that," Jessica spouted.

"Oh?"

Jessica turned and exited as calmly as she could. Charlotte would not control her. "Mrs. Blair," Jessica said, forcing herself to sound unemotional, "could you please give me the number for the district office? And do you know whom I would talk to about my file?"

The secretary scribbled down the information and handed the paper to Jessica. "I hope everything works out for you," Mrs. Blair whispered.

"Oh, it will," Jessica replied confidently. "It will."

Retreating to the teachers' lounge to use the phone, Jessica dialed the number and asked for the person listed on the paper.

"I'm sorry, she's gone for the day. Can someone else help you?"

"I hope so. I'm a new teacher at Glenbrooke High, and there seems to be a mix-up with my file. I didn't receive my paycheck today, and I need to know who can help me with that."

"One moment, please." The woman put Jessica on hold.

She waited a full three minutes before another voice came on the line. "Are you Jessica Morgan?"

"Yes, but I go by Jessica Fenton. There's been a bit of a mix-up, you see, and—"

"Right. We received a call yesterday from the principal at Glenbrooke. Can I ask you to give me your social security number?"

Jessica repeated her number, and the voice asked, "Have you changed the records with Social Security? Do they have you listed as Fenton or Morgan?"

Jessica could see this was going to be much more compli-cated than she ever imagined. Several people in this town already knew her as Jessica Morgan; maybe she should come out of hiding. "Let me ask you something. Would my paycheck still be held up if it was written in the name of Jessica Morgan?"

"No, since that's how you're registered with us. If you want it in Fenton, we need a written notice from you and a signed authorization from the principal to release the hold she has placed on your file. Plus it wouldn't hurt if you could provide us with your Oregon driver's license number."

"I don't have it yet." Jessica began to feel overwhelmed and weary of the whole mess. "Can you just go ahead and issue a check to me in the name of Jessica Morgan, and we'll leave it at that?"

"I think we can. The person in charge has already gone for the day, but we can cut the check on Monday and you'll receive it by Tuesday."

"Fine. Please do that." She hung up and left school as quickly as she could, taking long strides toward her house. Only instead of turning on her street, she kept walking. Her encounter with Charlotte had fueled her with so much anger that she hadn't walked it all off by the time she had reached her street. As she turned down the next street, she found herself headed for the cemetery. Then it occurred to her that, for two weeks, she had wanted to see the name on the gravestone where Kyle had placed the daisies. Now was a good time to take a look.

The cemetery gate was open. Jessica stepped inside its boundaries and felt as if she had walked across an invisible line into quiet and calm. The cemetery was like a lush park with towering trees filled with bird choirs. A stone bench stood a few yards to her left, and Jessica decided it would be a lovely place to come and sit one day and do some soul searching. But not today. Her interest took her to the right, not to the bench on the left.

The gravestone was easy to find. The daisies were all wilted, but around the headstone grew wild cornflowers and Queen Anne's lace. Jessica knelt and read the inscription, "Lindsey Sue Atkins. March 3, 1971-September 3, 1991. Loved by all. Safe in the arms of Jesus."

Atkins. Kyle's last name was Buchanan. Was she related to him? A former lover? Someone he rescued? How had she died?

Jessica was about to leave when she noticed the gravestone next to Lindsey's. It read, "Thelma Jean Atkins, beloved wife of Clyde Jacob Atkins. Born: January 7, 1909. Died:

November 14, 1991. Safe in the arms of Jesus."

She died only a few months after Lindsey. Did they die of the same thing? Were they related?

Jessica slowly walked away from the grave, finding that her curiosity had been heightened rather than satisfied. She went over to the stone bench and sat down. It was cold. She felt cold.

Some of the trees around her were just beginning to shake out their summer greens. Some of them were already adorning themselves with gold lace around the edges. The clouds covered the sun, and a few drops of rain found their way through the leafy maze overhead and plopped down next to Jessica, as if they had been invited. She didn't mind the company. She was thinking of her mom again.

Jessica realized that this was what she had missed all the years of growing up. A cemetery. A tombstone. A place to mourn her loss. She couldn't visit the cremated ashes that had been sprinkled into the Pacific Ocean. No marker existed in the ocean to read again and again and to remember.

Strangely, Jessica felt clearer about her mom's death than she ever had before. The gut wrenching cry of a few weeks ago must have done her good. This quiet bench was doing her good, too. She could come here and sit and remember whenever she needed to process the feelings she had kept inside for the past seventeen years.

Jessica closed her eyes and listened to the birds. The fresh smell of rain rising from the thick grass filled her nostrils and comforted her.

"Miss Fenton?" A gentle voice seemed to speak from out of nowhere.

Jessica snapped her eyes open and saw Dawn Laughlin standing in front of her. "Dawn, you startled me! I didn't hear you walk up."

"I saw you here and, well, if you don't mind, could I talk to you for a minute?" Dawn had on her purple and gold cheerleader's outfit, and her long bare legs were covered with goose bumps.

"Sure, but it's kind of chilly here."

"That's okay," Dawn said, sitting down on the cold stone bench next to Jessica. Dawn crossed her legs and folded her arms, tucking her hands under her upper arms and slouching so that her long, straight hair fell over her shoulders. Dawn looked younger than sixteen. Perhaps it was her round features. Her nose was round, so was her chin, her eyes, her face, and even her cheeks when she smiled. It made her look like a little girl.

"It's about something you said in class this week," Dawn began.

"Yes?" Jessica heard a truck engine and glanced over Dawn's shoulder toward the street. Dawn's bright yellow sports car was parked next to the cemetery's entrance, and right in front of it, Kyle's truck had pulled up and stopped. The engine was still running.

Jessica looked away, wondering if Kyle had seen her. She focused on Dawn. "What did you want to ask me?"

"You know that book you were reading from yesterday?"

Jessica thought back. "Oh, yes, *The Pardoners' Tale,* by Chaucer. I won't use any of it on the test, if that's what you're wondering. I was only reading it in the old English style to give the class an idea of how it sounded."

"Actually, what I was wondering was where you got the book. You said you bought your copy for fifty pence in a second-hand bookstore."

"That's right." Jessica couldn't imagine why Dawn was asking her about this. It had only been a fleeting comment. "It's my hobby; I collect antique books."

"Did you buy it in England?"

"Yes, in London. Why?"

Dawn's face lit up and her round brown eyes looked relieved. "So you've been to England."

"Yes."

"Have you been to Paris?" Dawn ventured.

"Yes."

"So have I," Dawn said. "My mom lives there."

"Yes, I heard that," Jessica said. She chanced a glance over Dawn's shoulder again and saw that Kyle's truck was still there but Kyle didn't seem to be in sight.

"This probably sounds totally stupid, but could I talk to you about Paris sometime?" Dawn asked. "See, nobody in this town has ever been anywhere. Well, except the ones who go on the Mexico trip with the church. That's different, though. It's like I have this whole other life because I spend summers with my mom, and I can't talk about it to anyone. Do you understand?"

"Yes, I think I do. I'd love to talk to you about Paris," Jessica said warmly. "My door is always open to you, Dawn. I live on Marigold Lane—the yellow two-story cottage with the white shutters."

"Yes, I know the house," Dawn said.

"You're welcome to come visit me any time."

Dawn popped up from the bench, a broad smile pushing her cheeks into their rosy, round posture. "I will. Thanks! I have to go."

"Bye," Jessica said, watching Dawn's cheerleader skirt swish as she jogged to her car. "Stop by anytime," Jessica called out.

Dawn waved, slid into her snazzy car, and zipped away. Jessica watched her go and strained her eyes to see if Kyle was still in the front seat of his truck. She couldn't tell. Now she had to make a decision. Should she leave, chancing an encounter with Kyle? Or should she stay here on this cold bench and wait to see where Kyle was?

Before she could decide, a rich, deep voice behind her said, "Hello, Jessica."

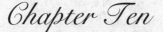

Chapter Ten

essica involuntarily jumped up and turned to face Kyle. At the first sight of his rugged jawline and clear green eyes, Jessica felt like a schoolgirl, all tongue-tied and self-conscious.

"I noticed you were talking with Dawn, and I didn't want to interrupt." Kyle wore that timid, little-boy look he had the morning he had visited her in the hospital. "I won't keep you. I just wanted to let you know that Ida asked me to come over and check that leak in your bathtub."

"Oh," Jessica said, picking up her purse and book bag as if she were about to make a dash for it. She remembered mentioning the leak briefly to Ida on Wednesday. Never had she guessed that Kyle would be the handyman assigned to look into the problem. "That's fine."

"Well, I wanted you to know that I can't get to it for a few days, maybe even a week."

"That's fine. No problem. Whenever." Jessica began to take a few steps backward.

"I'm going to Nevada for awhile." Kyle threw out the words as if he had no confidence that she would receive them. "I'm on a hot-shot team of firefighters. We leave tonight at six. I'm not sure when we'll be back."

Jessica vaguely remembered hearing about a wildfire in Nevada, along with another raging in Wyoming. "Oh, is the Nevada fire getting bad?" Her heart was still pounding hard and Jessica felt awkward trying to form a sentence.

"It's burned more than four hundred acres already. It's coming close to the town of Fallon. They've called on the Oregon teams because all their local hotshots went to Wyoming a few days ago." Kyle looked almost like a soldier going off to war who wasn't sure of his return.

Jessica didn't know what to say.

"So," Kyle concluded, taking a breath, "I'll look at your leaky bathtub when I come back."

In contrast to the drama of going off to fight a fire, a leaky tub seemed trivial. Jessica said, "Well, don't worry about it. It's not that bad, really."

A thick silence hung between them. The few sprinkles of rain that had escaped from the heavens during the past half hour were now joined by all their friends and relatives in a true drizzle. Jessica stood silently, the cold stone bench posted between her and Kyle. She wondered if he were going to ask if she wanted a ride home.

But he didn't.

He left, awkwardly, and she walked home alone in the rain.

That night, in the silence of her bedroom, tucked under her warm covers, Jessica listened to the rain falling steadily on her roof and thought how strange it was that Kyle was now in a very hot, dry place fighting a fire, while here, everything was cool and wet.

She didn't want to think about Kyle. She had done enough

of that in the past three weeks to last her a lifetime. What she needed to do was think about Jessica. She had enough of her own problems to work out without adding Kyle.

Food, once again, rose to the top. Could she last until Tuesday when her paycheck would supposedly arrive? She fell asleep dreaming of pork chops, baked potatoes, and DoveBars.

Late Saturday afternoon Jessica heard a knock on her front door. She left her papers on the mahogany secretary and padded to the door in her stocking feet.

"Hi. Is this a good time to visit?" Dawn asked, her round face puckered with a hesitant expression.

"Sure, come on in." Jessica motioned toward the living room. Dawn took a seat on the green couch, crossing and uncrossing her bare legs. It had rained off and on all day, but it wasn't particularly cold. Still, Jessica had on leggings, a long sweatshirt, and socks. Dawn wore sandals, shorts, and a denim shirt. Jessica still thought like a Southern Californian, who, when it rained, dressed warm, built a fire, and stayed inside all day. Oregonians apparently saw it as just another day.

"I'm afraid I don't have anything in the house to offer you to drink," Jessica said.

"That's okay. I'm not thirsty." Dawn gazed around the room, taking in the details. Jessica hadn't done much more decorating than to place a small vase of wild flowers on the dining room table.

"Were you writing letters?" Dawn asked, noticing the papers spread out on the secretary.

"Oh, no, it's just some notes and things." Jessica didn't feel comfortable telling Dawn that she was working on her *Under the Flowering Bush* story. She wished she had closed the desk up before answering the door. "So, tell me about Paris," she said, trying to change the conversation's focus.

"It's all right, I guess. The people are different from the

people here. More private. It's actually a lonely place for me. I think my mom is sort of lonely, too, only she would never admit that. She's too proud. She would never admit that she made a mistake when she ran away from home."

"Ran away?" Jessica asked, thinking it a humorous term to use in reference to a grown woman leaving her husband.

"She wanted the glamorous kind of life her sister had. My aunt married some rich guy, and my mom thought that was better than being married to a doctor, so she just left one day. We didn't know where she was for about a month. Then my dad received this letter, and he told me they were getting a divorce. About six months later my mom called me and said she was remarried and wanted me to spend the summer on the Riviera with them on his yacht."

"Did you have fun?"

"I didn't go. I told her I already had my summer planned. The next summer I went, though. And this past summer I went, too. It's like a movie in some ways, you know? The servants, the huge mansion, the yacht, and everything. But it's really lonely."

"I bet," Jessica said, trying to sound as sympathetic as she felt.

"It's just so false. I met this guy last summer. Giovanni. He was from Italy. He came to this party on the yacht one night and…" Dawn stopped and looked down at her knees. She didn't say anything else.

"Did Giovanni make you do something you didn't want to?" Jessica asked cautiously.

"Kind of," Dawn said, tears beginning to fall onto her tanned thighs. "I wanted him to kiss me, but then when he did, he wouldn't stop. I felt like such a baby. He was kissing me and touching me everywhere, and when he tried to unbutton my shirt, I ran away and locked myself in my room. It was so humiliating."

"I think you did the right thing," Jessica said softly. "You weren't ready."

"My mom thought I should be. She had a little talk with me the next morning," Dawn said, looking up and blinking back the tears. "All about 'protection' and 'being prepared.' She even gave me some…, well, you know, some of those things to carry in my purse."

Jessica waited for Dawn to continue.

"I'm just not ready," Dawn said.

"That's okay."

"But see, everybody seems to think I already have, you know, slept around. The guys at school treat me differently than they do the other girls. To be honest with you, I almost feel like going out and…" Dawn seemed to be searching for the right word. "And just getting it over with."

"You have to be true to who you really are, Dawn," Jessica said. "Only you can decide who that is and who that is going to be."

A hint of a smile pulled Dawn's lip up on the left side. "That's what I'm trying to figure out. And that's what I'm hoping you can help me figure out. See, it's like I said before, you don't seem like the other people in this town. You've been places. You know things. I can tell. You're experienced."

"Well, maybe not exactly the way you think, Dawn. Besides, you can't try to make your life like someone else's. You have to live your own life."

"I guess I'm looking for a model."

"A model?" Jessica felt uncomfortable. "Look, Dawn, I can be your teacher and even a good listener on the side. But I'm not anybody's role model, and I don't want to be." Jessica realized how abrupt and uncaring her words had come out. She wished she had formulated them better.

"Well, can I at least ask you one favor?"

"Of course," Jessica said, hoping that whatever it was, she would be able to say yes to it and make up for the way she had just pushed Dawn aside.

"It's kind of a big favor." Dawn paused and looked into Jessica's eyes. "Would you go on this trip to Mexico with the church group?"

Jessica laughed aloud. "Mexico? Why would you want me to go to Mexico?"

"It's only for four days," Dawn said. "And I'm going this year because I want to see what I'm made of."

"I think that's great, but you certainly don't need me to go for you to find that out."

"I don't have a lot of friends," Dawn said the words carefully. "I mean, a lot of people act like they want to hang out with me, but they don't really understand me. You see, this trip is a pretty big deal for me, and I'd really like it if you were there."

Jessica tried to understand what Dawn was saying, the unspoken message behind the words. She knew some of those insecure feelings of growing up and trying to make decisions when you're the only child at home, when you live with a father who is too busy to notice you, and when you wish every day you had a mom to talk to. Yes, Jessica understood Dawn's feelings. Still, it wasn't enough to convince Jessica she should go to Mexico.

"Dawn, I appreciate you asking me to go to Mexico with you, but it's just not possible."

"Why not? The chaperons have their way paid for them. There's no school on Friday, and Monday is a holiday. I know you would have a good time."

Jessica shook her head. "Sorry. I can't go."

Dawn let out an exasperated puff of air. "Will you at least think about it and pray about it?"

Jessica pursed her lips together and felt the scar tissue on her top lip tighten as she did. "I'll think about it."

Dawn's face lit up. "Thanks."

She really is a pretty girl, Jessica thought. *I'd hate to see her mess up her life.*

Dawn changed the subject to school and told Jessica how their guys had won the football game last night. The two of them visited for another five or ten minutes before Jessica asked Dawn a question she didn't think she could ask anyone else in town. "I happened to notice a grave yesterday across from where I was sitting. The name was Lindsey Atkins. Did you know her?"

"Lindsey? She was Thelma's granddaughter. She came down from Spokane to take care of Thelma after Thelma got cancer. Lindsey was only here about five months, and then she got pneumonia or something, and she died. It was a big shock to everyone."

Jessica nodded, hoping Dawn would continue.

"She was so pretty. Red hair and pale skin. She had the most beautiful voice. They had this dinner for the hospital that my dad took me to once, and after dinner Lindsey sang all these Irish songs. I was only in the seventh grade, but I remember it really well."

"She sounds as if she were a lovely woman," Jessica said. "How sad that she died when she was only twenty years old."

"I think the saddest part was that she and Kyle had just gotten engaged. Do you know Kyle Buchanan? He's a firefighter here."

Jessica tried to keep her expression steady. "Yes, I've met Kyle."

"They were totally in love, from what everybody says. When she died, Kyle took a leave of absence from his job and moved in with Thelma. He took care of her until the day she died, as if she were his own grandma."

"Well," was all Jessica could say. *What a kind man to care for an elderly, dying woman. How deep his love for Lindsey must have been.*

"My dad said once that the whole thing made Kyle paranoid, or something like that."

"What did he mean?" Jessica asked.

"I don't know. I guess Kyle hasn't gone out with anybody since Lindsey died."

After Dawn left, Jessica thought of how long she had gone on with her life and failed to mourn for the loss of her mother. Perhaps Dr. Laughlin would call her paranoid too, but for the opposite reason. Kyle had mourned too long, and she had just begun.

That evening she sat alone again with the old photo album and cried over her mother's photos—not the painful, gut wrenching kind of tears she had cried a few weeks ago. This time her tears were like a steady, gentle rain that brought with it a cleansing and healing of the heart. And that was enough to get her through the weekend.

She thought constantly about Kyle and watched the news at six and eleven for updates on the fire. Was he safe? Would the fire be contained soon? The reports Sunday night said that more than a thousand acres had burned, the fire was twenty percent contained, and no homes had been destroyed.

How much longer would Kyle be there? She thought of his dark brown hair and the way it turned wavy on top. She thought of the way his steady hand had felt on her lip in the ambulance and the scent of his cinnamon gum. So her weekend went, with thoughts of Kyle and food filling most of it.

On Monday, she decided to give her students a writing assignment. She was too hungry to concentrate on lecturing. "Okay, take out a sheet of paper," Jessica instructed, "and write a description of a person you know well. Use the five senses in your descriptions and give me at least three paragraphs."

Jessica sat down, and her stomach grumbled loudly. She hoped no one heard. After class she planned to raid the faculty lounge for donuts, coffee, anything.

But all she found were rice cakes. With no one watching, Jessica ate the whole bag. She told herself that tomorrow she would have that paycheck and the first thing she would do was buy herself a DoveBar and some treats for the faculty to replace all she had consumed in the past few weeks.

However, on Tuesday, the check didn't show up in her box. After school she made another dreaded trip to the office. She had listed her Aunt Bonnie as her nearest relative. Aunt Bonnie and Uncle John lived in Pennsylvania. She had little contact with them, but still, that was the best she could do for a relative.

"Looking for something?" Charlotte questioned when Jessica stepped into the office.

Jessica didn't say anything. She just returned the stare Charlotte gave her.

"Here it is," Charlotte said, producing the white envelope from behind her back. "Before I give this to you," Charlotte said, drawing the envelope toward her face and tapping it against the side of her cheek, "I want you to know that I'm on to you, Ms. Morgan."

Jessica's heart froze. She mechanically covered up any emotion.

"I don't know what little game you're playing or who you are or what you're doing here in Glenbrooke, but I'm on your trail, and I intend to find out. Because, you see, women who have a degree from Oxford don't become high school English teachers in small towns unless they're hiding from something. The law, maybe?"

Jessica snatched her check from Charlotte's hand and turned to march off.

"You just wait. I'm going to find out what you're hiding," Charlotte called after her.

Jessica's long strides took her through the front door and down the steps two at a time. She heard a beep-beep. Teri's car was parked at the curb.

"Hop in," Teri called.

Jessica was too steamed to do anything else. She plopped down in the seat and shut the door hard.

"Get your check?"

"Finally!" Jessica spouted. "What *is* that woman's problem?"

"Oh, don't let her get to you. Let's go to the bank. Where's your account?"

"I don't have one yet," Jessica said.

"I know just the place then." Teri turned a corner and headed for the center of town. She turned on the radio and started to sing the pop song that filled the air around them.

Her cheery disposition had a diffusing effect on Jessica's anger, and by the time they reached the bank, Jessica felt somewhat recovered from her encounter with Charlotte.

"I need two forms of ID," the bank manager said as she began to type up Jessica's form.

"Um, that's kind of a problem," Jessica said. "I don't have any with me."

"Not even a driver's license? It can be out of state."

"No, I don't have anything with me."

The woman stopped typing. "I'm sorry. I can't complete this without some form of ID. Would you like to stop by tomorrow with your identification, and we can finish this up?"

"Okay," Jessica said numbly. She hadn't thought of this

hitch. What would she tell Teri, who was over at a teller's window talking to someone she knew?

"That was fast," Teri said.

"I wasn't able to open the account. I need a driver's license first. Is the DMV nearby?"

"It's not far, but they'll be closed in a few minutes. We'll have to come back tomorrow."

As they walked to Teri's car, a goblin of panic began to howl inside Jessica's head. How was she going to wait until tomorrow to get some food? "Teri, do you have one of those check cashing stores here? You know, the kind where they charge you a fee, but they don't require ID?"

"I know what you're talking about," Teri said. "We had a lot of those in Escondido. Glenbrooke is too small for something like that. Do you need to borrow some money until you cash your check?"

Jessica hesitated. Her pride overpowered her. "No, that's okay. Thanks."

"Where do you want me to take you?" Teri asked.

To the store, to a Dairy Queen, to your house—anywhere that has food! Jessica thought. All that came out of her mouth, was, "Home, I guess."

It was quiet for a minute, and then Teri said, "You know what, Jessica? Even though everything has been kind of a struggle for you since you arrived—the accident, Charlotte, not having a car, and whatever else—I just know that God is watching over you. I think everything is going to turn out fine."

Jessica couldn't help but snort her disbelief.

"It's kind of hard to trust God sometimes, isn't it?" Teri asked cautiously.

"Let's just say that I live with the philosophy that God helps those who help themselves."

"I don't think it works that way," Teri said, turning the corner to Jessica's street. "The way I see it is that when we surrender
to God, he comes in and acts in awesome ways."

"Awesome ways?"

"You know what I mean. He supernaturally works everything out for the best."

Jessica didn't have the strength to argue with Teri over her
version of the supernatural or her opinion of what God's best
might be. They pulled up in front of Jessica's house and both
noticed three paper bags sitting by the front door.

Jessica reached them first and peered inside. They were full
of groceries. From the looks of it, they had just been delivered
because the frozen can of orange juice on top was still frosty.
The accompanying note simply said, "Welcome to
Glenbrooke."

"What's in the bags?" Teri asked, trotting up the walkway
to join Jessica.

"Groceries," Jessica said in a matter-of-fact tone. Inside, she
was flabbergasted.

"Who left them?"

"I don't know." Jessica showed Teri the note.

A smile spread across Teri's face, and she said, "See what I
mean? This is God's awesome way. You weren't able to go to the
store today, so God brought the store to you."

Jessica unlocked the door and lifted the first bag. "I
wouldn't exactly say I was surrendered to anything or anybody, which you said was the prerequisite." Jessica prided herself on having done everything herself so far and not letting
anyone have control of her life.

"Then I'd call this a cushion of grace. God knew what you
needed and provided it before you even had a chance to ask
him for it. He caught you on his cushion of grace before you
fell." Teri carried the other two bags into the kitchen and

placed them on the counter. "I need to use your restroom. Then I'll help you unload your awesome groceries. Where is your bathroom, anyhow?"

"Upstairs," Jessica said. The minute Teri left the room, Jessica began to breathe deeply, trying to hold back her tears of amazement.

She lifted a rump roast from the sack and pressed the tender red meat with her thumbs. Her mouth began to water. She couldn't remember the last time she had eaten beef. It must have been that Dairy Queen burger three weeks ago with Kyle. Next came a bag of carrots and then potatoes, milk, eggs, butter, cheese, bread, chicken, lettuce, canned soup, spices, juice, peaches, apples, coffee, broccoli, and then, at the bottom of the last bag, there it was. Jessica couldn't believe her eyes as she lifted out a box of DoveBars.

She began to cry silently and clutched the frozen box to herself like it was a precious gift. Who knew? She hadn't said a word about her DoveBar dreams to anyone. Who could have possibly known that of all the things they could have bought for her at the grocery store, this was the ultimate prize. Who knew? God? Jessica brushed the thought away the moment it appeared. A God who would provide her with all this food and even include DoveBars would destroy her firmly established image of God as a vengeful party pooper.

"What a haul!" Teri said brightly, stepping back into the kitchen.

Jessica blinked away her tears and discretely set the box of DoveBars on the counter with the rest of the food.

"What do you want me to put away?" Teri asked. "The refrigerator stuff?"

Before Jessica could stop her, Teri opened the refrigerator and froze with the same stunned look that Kyle had had. "Boy," Teri said with a laugh, "you really were low on groceries." She opened the freezer door and had the same surprised reaction. "I'd say these groceries arrived just in time!" Teri started to fill the refrigerator shelves with the bounty.

Jessica opened a cupboard door and started to stack the soup cans and spaghetti noodles rapidly on the shelves, hoping Teri wouldn't notice the cupboard had been empty. Teri noticed.

"Looks as if you were out of everything." Teri's perky voice had been replaced by a serious one. "Jess, how long have you been out of food?"

"Not long," Jessica said, feeling trapped and nervous. Did she dare lower her guard and talk to Teri honestly? It had been so long since she had felt free to say what she really thought or felt to anyone. All her words had been so guarded.

Teri stopped putting away the food. Standing next to Jessica, she asked, "How long, Jess? Yesterday? The day before?"

Jessica didn't answer.

"I thought we were friends, Jessica. Friends can trust each other. Friends can tell each other when they're going through a rough time. I want to be your friend. Will you please let me into your life? Will you just tell me the truth, Jessica?"

"The truth is," Jessica began slowly, still controlling her emotions, "I ran out of food, and I've been waiting for my paycheck so I could go to the grocery store. That's all. I really don't appreciate you talking to me like I'm some kind of child."

"That's not how I mean to sound," Teri said. "I apologize if that's how I came across to you." She hesitated, then apparently realizing that was the best answer Jessica was going to give, Teri returned to her task and silently put away the rest of the groceries.

As soon as they were all in place and the paper bags were folded, Teri said, "Well, I guess I'll be going. I'll see you tomorrow." She headed for the door, then stopped and turned around. "Oh, and if you want a ride to the DMV, it's no problem. I'd be glad to take you right after school."

"Great," Jessica said. "I'll see you tomorrow. Thanks!"

Once Teri was out the door, Jessica lunged for the freezer, removed the box of DoveBars, ripped it open, pulled out a bar, yanked off the paper wrapper, and slowly, solemnly took a bite. The ice cream and chocolate melted in her mouth exactly the way she knew it would. She had waited so long for this moment. It was delicious.

With a flinch of pain she regretted not having a friend to share this joyful moment with. But that, she knew, had been the price she had to pay if she were to keep her secret.

Chapter Eleven

or the next week or so Jessica ate like a queen and felt optimistic about her life. She had an Oregon driver's license, a bank account with money in it, relatively few hassles from Charlotte, and a growing awareness of how much Dawn admired her.

Jessica had managed to keep Teri at arm's length, yet maintain their friendship. She was grateful for Teri's cheery hellos each day and her "taxi" services available to Jessica without any hint of it being an imposition for Teri. But Jessica especially appreciated that Teri didn't push the issue about the food or the insinuation that Jessica hadn't trusted her enough to tell her what was going on.

The only thing Teri bugged Jessica about was the aloe vera plant. Jessica had confessed to trying the gel only once and wasn't sure it had done any good. Teri said it took regular use and started checking with Jessica everyday to see if she was smearing the gel on her lip.

Kyle was gone the whole week, fighting the Nevada fire.

And every night, when Jessica was alone, she was fighting the Kyle-fire spreading in her heart. Ever since she had learned of Lindsey and how Kyle cared for her grandmother after Lindsey died, Jessica felt growing inside of her a deep spirit of compassion toward Kyle. Somehow, his act of mercy to this woman soothed Jessica's pain about the loss of her own mother in an inexplicable way.

In the still, fresh crispness of each new day as Jessica walked to school, she found herself haunted, not by the memory of her mother or all the complications she had left behind when she came to Glenbrooke. It was Kyle's face she saw in the clouds. His rich, soothing voice she heard on the wind. And it was sheer torture.

Kyle was still fighting the Nevada fire on September 28, the day Charlotte had arranged for him to speak at their assembly. One of the other firefighters, Bobbie, gave the presentation instead. Jessica noticed that Charlotte didn't stay in the auditorium after she introduced him.

Charlotte had her hands full lately, which meant she was paying less attention to Jessica and even seemed to have forgotten her vow to uncover Jessica's mysterious past. Charlotte was preoccupied because, in a fit of anger, Monday morning she had fired Mrs. Blair and was frantically trying to find a replacement. Some of the teachers said it was actually Mrs. Blair who quit and walked out. Of course, with Glenbrooke being a small town, Charlotte's reputation was well established, making it difficult to find a new secretary.

On the first Monday of October, Jessica was in middle of her third class, discussing the opening line of *Mirabeau* from the essays of Thomas Carlyle, when someone walked past her open classroom door. She thought for sure it was Kyle.

Trying to focus her attention back on the class, she asked, "Can someone tell me what you think the first line means?"

Bill raised his hand. Jessica liked Bill. Tall, lean, with round glasses and a quick wit, Bill always found a way to make the class laugh. He was a bit of a country boy. She had seen him in cowboy boots more than once and expected him to show up wearing a cowboy hat any day now. Jessica looked forward to her third class each day, knowing that Bill would be there to liven things up. "Yes, Bill?"

"It means we're not done yet." He pressed his finger onto the top of his head the way a cook checks the center of a cake to see if it's done. "Nope. Still too squishy." The class laughed.

"Okay," Jessica agreed with Bill's conclusion. "But what about the outward appearance? It says, 'The house that is a-building looks not as the house that is built.' What does Carlyle mean by 'looks not'?"

Bill popped off again with, "Because a building looks like a building, and a house looks like a house. Buildings are buildings, and houses are houses. Didn't you ever watch children's instructional television, ma'am?"

"This was written in 1837, as I already mentioned. What word do we use today instead of 'a-building?'"

"High-rise?" Bill ventured. The class laughed.

"How about 'under construction?'" Jessica asked. "How are people under construction?"

"It's like I said," Bill volunteered. "We're not done yet."

Realizing that was the best she was going to get from this bunch, she instructed them to read the rest of the essay in class and answer the questions on the handout she had prepared for them.

The class became relatively quiet as the students began their reading assignment, or at least appeared to be working on their assignment. Jessica found an excuse to wander to the back of the room where she would be next to the open door, in case it was Kyle she had seen and he walked by again. She

SECRETS

pretended to be looking through a box on the back shelf and thought how she was just as bad as the students. They were appearing to be reading, but she knew that many of them were finding other, more interesting things to do. She glanced at Bill, who seemed to be extra busy with a piece of paper and a felt pen. "Make good use of your time, class," Jessica said. "This will be due tomorrow."

A few muffled groans rippled across the room. Jessica checked the clock. Five more minutes until class was over, and then she had a break. She would have to meander somewhere and see if Kyle was around campus today. If she saw him, she didn't know what she would say. It was too intriguing though, not to see if he had returned from the wild fire. If he was here, was it on his own or due to another of Charlotte's requests?

The bell rang. The students bolted from their seats, and the hallways filled with boisterous teens. Jessica stood by the doorway, smiling as each student rushed by her. She liked her students. They were a surprising source of energy and encouragement to her.

Among the last to leave was Bill. He had a handwritten sign made from notebook paper and hung with two rubber bands around his neck. He shuffled past her as if he didn't really care if she stopped him and read the note or not, but of course she did. It said, "Pardon our dust. We're still under construction." The "under construction" part was marked out, and above it in old English letters he had written, "a-building."

Jessica laughed, as did the three other students standing around Bill. "I'm so glad you learned something today, Bill."

Bill looked over the top of Jessica's head, and a big smile spread across his face. "Hey, Kyle! When did you get back?"

Jessica caught her breath and made herself turn around slowly. Yes, it was definitely the face she had seen in her dreams

134

for the past week. Kyle had on jeans and a denim work shirt with the sleeves rolled up.

"Last night," Kyle said, answering Bill but looking at Jessica.

She wanted to wrap her arms around those broad shoulders, press her cheek against that no-nonsense jaw, and whisper in his ear that she was so glad, so relieved he was home safe from the fire.

"Hi," was all she said. The faint scent of cinnamon hung in the air between them.

"Teri tells me you want to go to Mexico with us this weekend," Kyle said.

Jessica was speechless.

"Cool!" Bill said. "You're going to love it! The people in the village are awesome. This will be my third time going. Hey, does Dawn know you're going?"

Bill took off down the hall in search of Dawn, the under construction sign still hanging around his neck.

"I…," Jessica looked up into Kyle's green eyes. He looked tired. "I don't know."

Suddenly Dawn was at her elbow. "Are you really going with us?"

"Well…"

"I've been trying to talk her into it, Kyle," Dawn said. Turning to Jessica she added in a lower voice, "You have to go. It's going to be my first time, too. If I can do this, you can."

Out of the corner of her eye, Jessica saw Teri step outside her classroom door and then duck back inside the minute she noticed Jessica with Kyle.

I'm going to get her for this!

"Our final meeting is tonight at church," Kyle said, apparently aware of the awkwardness of the situation. "Seven o'clock."

"She'll be there," Dawn said. "She's coming."

"It's up to you," Kyle said. "I have to get going. Is it okay if I call you later about repairing the bathtub?"

Bathtub? "Oh, right. The leak in the bathtub. Sure. Any time. I'll be home. I don't think the leak will be going anywhere." She smiled weakly at her attempt at a joke.

Kyle smiled, said good-bye to Jessica and Dawn, and then fearlessly merged into the flow of hallway traffic, a full head and shoulders above most of the kids. Lots of students recognized Kyle and said hi or slapped him a high five. The bell rang, and the students scattered to their classrooms. Except for Dawn. She stood next to Jessica, her round eyes pleading, and her full lips turned down in a slight pout.

"Oh, all right!" Jessica finally said. "I'll at least go to the meeting at your church tonight. Then I'll decide."

Dawn's face lit up. "Peachy!"

"Peachy?" Jessica repeated.

"Yeah, peachy! I'll see you tonight."

Jessica nodded, and Dawn hurried down the hall, late for her next class. With determined steps, Jessica marched into Teri's class and stood in the back with her hands on her hips as Teri wrote seven Spanish verbs on the board. Teri spotted Jessica and asked the class to take out a piece of paper and conjugate the verbs without any talking. Then she joined Jessica and directed her out into the hallway.

"Truce?" was all Teri said.

"Why did you do it?" Jessica asked. "Why did you tell him I would go?"

"Because he asked if I'd found another chaperon, and I told him you were the only one I've talked to about the trip. And you are. I don't know anyone else who would be good to take on a trip like this."

"How can you be so sure I would be good to take?" Jessica

asked. It wasn't that she was mad at Teri, but she didn't like the thought that she had been coerced into the trip. She refused to be forced into anything.

"Look," Teri said, "I feel like God has something for you on this trip. Sorry if I overstepped my boundaries."

"You *feel* like God has something for me? Is this another one of your supernatural 'awesome' things? Because that's not how I make decisions. It's not good enough to just 'feel' something. I don't base anything on my feelings," Jessica said firmly.

"I know," Teri said, looking solemn. "And that's too bad."

Teri's words felt like a slap to Jessica. Who was Teri to evaluate Jessica's belief and behavior system and find it unacceptable?

A rumble of students' voices began to filter though the doorway. Teri looked in on her class. "I have to go. Can we talk about this after school?"

By the time school was over, Dawn had told several of the other teens that Jessica was thinking about going to Mexico. Each one of them dropped by her classroom and pleaded with her to come. Bill stopped by and told Jessica all the reasons he thought it would be a great idea for her to go to Mexico and then promptly presented a petition signed by a dozen or so students saying they wanted Jessica on the trip. It was nearly impossible to say no to Bill's cool persuasion. Jessica wondered if any young girls had found that out yet.

"You're not mad, then?" Teri asked as she and Jessica drove to the meeting that night.

"I'm still deciding."

"Deciding if you're mad at me, or deciding if you're going on the trip?"

"Both."

Teri's good-natured laugh bubbled over. "Can't you think of at least one good reason you should go?"

Jessica *did* have a good reason. Kyle. It surprised her that she would admit that to herself. "For Dawn's sake, I guess."

"There you go," Teri said. She parked the car and turned off the engine. "Hold that thought, okay?"

Jessica turned to open her passenger door and jumped when she saw Bill's face pressed up against her closed window with his mouth open like a fish. She opened the door, and Bill peeled himself off the moving window.

"How did you like my impression of a dead bug on the window?"

"Very realistic," Jessica said.

"Thank you, thank you," Bill said.

The three of them entered the double doors on the side of the church building and walked into a large, multi-purpose room. Teri led the way down a hall to the only room with lights on. About a dozen teenagers in the room were involved in lively conversations. Jessica scanned the room, recognizing all but three of the teens. Kyle stood in the corner, talking to a parent, and Dawn sat alone toward the back of the room. The minute Jessica entered, Dawn stood up with a bright smile and hurried to greet Jessica.

"I was worried you would change your mind," Dawn said, motioning for Jessica to follow her and sit with her. "I decided that if you didn't show up, I was going to leave and forget the whole thing."

They sat down, and Jessica said, "Dawn, you shouldn't depend on me so much. You need to make decisions for yourself."

"You don't understand," Dawn said softly. "That's all I do every day. I decide what I'm going to wear, what I'm going to eat, where I'm going to go after school. And I do everything by myself. I didn't want to go on this trip alone. Can you understand that?"

Jessica understood. Maybe even more than she wanted to.

The strength of her empathy with Dawn made her feel vulnerable.

Kyle finished with the parent and called the group together to start the meeting. He spotted Jessica and looked at her for what seemed to be longer than necessary. His look made her wonder if he had thought about her while he was in Nevada. Had he noticed her outfit tonight? She had changed four times and then sat on her bed and laughed at herself. Why was she expending so much effort when she supposedly didn't care about impressing Kyle? She had ended up pulling on a pair of jeans and black scoop neck T-shirt, which she wore tucked in with a wide belt. Very basic. And that's how she would act toward Kyle. Very basic. Natural and unpretentious.

As the meeting progressed, Jessica noticed how comfortable Kyle was with the teens. Even more comfortable than she felt as their teacher. He didn't seem to pay any special attention to her as he went through the list of what everyone needed to bring and what time their flight left on Friday from Portland.

A horrible thought came to Jessica. What if Kyle didn't want her to go on this trip? When he was at school he hadn't said anything along the lines of, "I hope you can come" or "It would great if you would come." He hadn't volunteered any personal commentary on his feelings.

Maybe I've been thinking about him and daydreaming for so long that I want to believe he wants me around him. And maybe I've decided that I want to be around him, and so I've talked myself into it.

Jessica thought about how she had treated him the last time he was in her home, ordering him out of her house and her life. What had changed in her heart and mind since then? Why did she want this relationship now?

What if it's too late? What if he wrote me off that afternoon? What if I've blown the one chance I had?

Chapter Twelve

The teens going on the Mexico trip huddled in a circle in the church parking lot on Friday morning, bracing themselves against the early morning chill. It was barely sunrise. Jessica could see her breath when she slipped out of Teri's car and joined the huddle.

"How about some help loading up this luggage?" Kyle asked from the back of his white truck. "Form a firefighter's brigade," he suggested.

The group shuffled into position and passed the sleeping bags and other gear from one person to the next. Bill was the one who ended up at the back of the truck, handing everything up to Kyle. With each piece of luggage came a comment.

"Whoa! Heads up! Cannonball! Comin' at ya'!"

Jessica noticed how Bill's attitude quickly infiltrated the rest of the group, and as the final pieces of luggage went into the truck, everyone had a joke to make. Even Teri.

She lifted her large duffel bag and said, "Here you go. This is my cosmetics bag." Everyone knew by looking at Teri that she was about as natural as they come.

It helped that the mood was light, because the sky certainly wasn't, and Jessica's emotions weren't either. She had almost backed out the night before and told Kyle and Teri that she had changed her mind. The only problem was she didn't know how she could tell Dawn. Whether motivated by guilt or insanity, Jessica was here, and she was about to spend the next four days in Mexico.

"Hey, you guys," Kyle called out as he hopped down from the back of the truck. "Let's pray, and then we need to hit the road if we're going to make that 9:30 flight out of Portland."

Jessica liked the way Kyle handled the students. She also liked the way he looked. A little bit sleepy. His hair a little bit wild. His grin a little bit crooked. She knew he had to be tired after returning from that intense fire and then having only a few days to pull everything together for this trip.

The group gathered in a lopsided circle, and Kyle prayed. Kyle sounded a lot like Teri when he prayed, as if he was talking to a real person, someone approachable and not distant like the God Jessica was acquainted with.

"Amen, amen," the teens all echoed when Kyle finished. It seemed like a secret handshake, something they all did automatically. Dawn was the only one who looked like an outsider.

They all climbed into a van, which was being driven to the airport by one of the dads. Jessica sat in the front bench seat, and Dawn slid in next to her. Kyle came over to the van, looked in the front window, and fixed his gaze on Jessica. She wondered if he would treat her any differently from the rest of the group.

He had called her two days before to apologize that he wouldn't be able to repair the tub before the Mexico trip.

Jessica had told him it could wait and that was about the extent of their conversation.

"Does anyone want to ride in the truck with me?" Kyle asked, looking at Jessica.

"I do!" a short girl from the back of the van shouted. She quickly vacated her seat, crawled out of the van, and hot footed it over to the truck.

"Do you have room for one more?" Bill asked.

"Sure," Kyle said, still gazing at Jessica.

"I'll go with you," Bill volunteered. He was still outside the van, filming the loading of the group with his video camera. "This is Wild Bill signing off until next time." He clicked off the camera and hurried to take his seat next to the cute girl already seated in the front of Kyle's truck.

Jessica kept her nonchalant gaze on Kyle as he jogged back over to his truck. He had on shorts and a gray sweatshirt. He looked good. How was she ever going to keep her focus on the kids this weekend with Kyle around all the time? She didn't imagine she would make a very good chaperon.

The ride to Portland took several hours. Jessica leaned against the window and tried to sleep. It was impossible. She ended up listening in on the conversations flowing around her. One thing she noticed was that these teens appeared to be stronger morally than a lot of the other students in her classes. It showed up in their dialogue and even in the way they treated each other. She had found out from Teri they took this trip over the weekend of Columbus Day because the first year they had gone over Thanksgiving and too many families had protested about their kids being absent from family celebrations.

Jessica imagined Dawn didn't have that problem. Single dads, in Jessica's experience, didn't tend to make much of a to-do over holidays.

Jessica's thoughts floated back to one particular Christmas when she was in high school. Her dad had taken off for the week with his latest girlfriend, and Jessica had stayed home alone. Since that time, Christmas and other holidays meant pain and isolation to Jessica.

She longed for her own life where she could oversee the celebrations. She pictured herself living in Oregon and putting on a feast at Thanksgiving that would mirror a Norman Rockwell picture of turkey dinner with all the trimmings and a dozen smiling faces around the table. Now that she was in Oregon, the question was, "Who are those smiling faces supposed to be?" She had consistently cut herself off from relationships and held people at arm's length since the day she had arrived. Who would want to come to her Thanksgiving dinner? Teri maybe? Dawn? Could she possibly invite Kyle?

The van came to a halt at a stoplight. Jessica opened her eyes and saw a sign that said, "Welcome to PDX." They were at the airport already, and she made herself admit that during the entire drive she had cut herself off from everyone.

I have to change. I must find a way to open up a little. I can't go on like this the rest of my life. I'll only become more lonely, and that's not what I want. I have to change! But how can I as long as I'm harboring my secret?

Jessica made a supreme effort to be more open on the airplane ride to San Diego. Dawn sat by her again. Jessica asked all kinds of questions. It was a way for her to establish contact without revealing anything about herself. In their conversation, Dawn mentioned that she was struggling with her Christianity, and she asked Jessica if she ever struggled.

"I'm not sure I know what you mean," Jessica said.

"I became a Christian about a year ago, but it's a lot harder than I thought it would be."

"What do you mean you became a Christian? How do you 'become' a Christian?"

Dawn looked a little surprised at Jessica's question. "You know, you give your life over to God. You ask him to forgive all your sins, and you surrender everything to him." Then, as if this had been a pop quiz question, Dawn added, "That's right, isn't it?"

"I'm asking you what you believe," Jessica said, putting the responsibility back on Dawn.

"That's what I believe," Dawn said firmly. "It's just that it's hard sometimes. That's why I wanted to go on this trip so much. I wanted to prove that I'm into God and Christianity and everything. A lot of people at school think I'm a party girl, but I'm not really. I guess I feel like I know what's right, but I still sort of stand on the edge a lot of times."

Jessica didn't feel she had any advice for Dawn. In some ways, Dawn seemed to have her goals and beliefs more clearly defined than Jessica. The "becoming a Christian" part of Dawn's answer confused her. Jessica considered herself to be a Christian. It was something she was born with, the way some people are born Jewish or Italian. Christianity was a part of her Caucasian heritage, not something she decided to become.

Once the group arrived in San Diego, the fun began. Kyle had rented a fifteen-passenger van and a small U-Haul truck, which were waiting for them at the airport. All their luggage and extra gear were thrown into the back of the truck, and the teens climbed into the van. The luggage overflowed the back of the truck, and Bill volunteered to climb in and squash everything so it would fit.

"Human horizontal bungee jumper!" Bill shouted and then slammed himself into a mound of sleeping bags.

"Careful!" Teri warned. "The ice chests are underneath all that."

"You're just worried about your cosmetic bag, Miss Moreno," Bill teased. "Hey, somebody get my camera. This is great footage."

One of the guys retrieved the small video camera from Bill's bag in the van and began to film the squashing of the luggage. Jessica had a feeling this videotaping of every little event was something they would be plagued with for the trip's duration.

Joel, the guy handling Bill's camera at the moment, turned the lens on Jessica and said, "And how about you, Miss Fenton? Are you ready for the mysteries and perils that lie in wait for us in the remote regions of the Mexicali Valley?"

Jessica looked away from the camera and caught Teri's smiling face focused on her. "Mexico?" Jessica said with mock horror. "Teri, I thought you said we were going to Maui!"

Everyone laughed. Joel turned the camera on Teri and said, "Do you have a comment to make, Miss Moreno, regarding Miss Fenton's accusation?"

"As a matter of fact, I do," Teri said. Joel focused the camera in for a close-up of her face. With a mischievous grin, Teri began to rattle off a string of Spanish words, ending with a perky, "*¿bueno?*"

"No fair!" Bill said. "All comments for the camera must be in English."

"Oh, come on," Teri said. "You, of all my students, should be able to understand what I said."

"Oh no," Bill groaned. Joel focused the camera on him. "Ladies and Gentlemen," Bill said in his mock announcer's voice, "we are about to enter the 'Bueno Zone,' where unsuspecting second-year Spanish students like myself suddenly find themselves required to spout entire phrases in a foreign tongue. We warn all you kids watching us out there, *don't* try this at home!"

Kyle came around the side of the van and caught the last

ROBIN JONES GUNN

few lines of Bill's monologue. "You guys ready to hit the road?"

"We could, but it might hurt our hands," Bill quipped.

"Come on, get in the van," Kyle said. He tossed a set of keys to Teri and said, "You ready?"

"Sure. Jess, you want to ride with me?" Teri asked.

She really wanted to ride with Kyle and the other crazy guys in the van. "Okay," Jessica heard herself say. She noticed that Kyle was looking at her again. *How that man's look haunts me! How does he do that? One look, and I turn into a big marshmallow.*

Everyone found a seat, and the caravan began the long, hot journey. When they arrived in Calexico, the city on the American side of the border, Kyle dropped off the group at a Burger King while he and a couple of the guys made a run to a hardware store. They bought an odd assortment of lumber, paint, and supplies for their building project. It took another hour of driving beyond the border to reach the village.

Jessica had expected poverty and dirty villages the moment they crossed over to the Mexican side, but she was amazed by the huge industrial buildings and modern stores in Mexicali, the Mexican border town. The buses, which rambled a little too close to their truck on the narrow roads, looked archaic though. One of them looked as if it might fall apart any minute and the dozens of passengers inside would come spilling out.

When they finally pulled into the village of Nueva, it was nearly dusk. Teri nodded and smiled at the people who stood outside their simple wooden or adobe homes. They all waved to Teri and Jessica, and from out of nowhere, dozens of children came running and squealing toward the van. Some young boys hopped onto the van's rear bumper as Kyle drove slowly over the rough dirt road to the center of the quaint village.

"Shouldn't you tell them to get off?" Jessica asked Teri. "It's so dangerous!"

"It's sort of their way of welcoming us," Teri said. "I think they're okay. Kyle knows they're back there."

A barefoot girl with her front two teeth missing came running up alongside the truck and grasped Teri's arm, which she had hung out the open window. "Ana Maria!" Teri cried out in recognition. "*¿Cómo estás, mi chica?*"

The endearing little girl held Teri's arm and trotted alongside them the rest of the way, chattering happily. It was a touching scene. Jessica could understand why Teri said earlier that many of these kids look forward to them coming down from year to year the way American kids look forward to Christmas.

Jessica had seen the boxes of clothing, toys, and Bibles the church had collected and was sending down with Kyle and his team. In a way, Jessica did feel like a Santa Claus. These kids had so little.

They pulled up in front of a partially finished building and parked the van and truck. The minute they stepped out of the vehicles, dozens of dirty little arms wrapped around each of the Americans, and a jabbering chorus of excited children filled the air. To her surprise, three little girls immediately attached themselves to Jessica, hugging her and looking up at her with glistening brown eyes. They all spoke to her with rapid words that sounded like they could be questions. Jessica could only shrug her shoulders and smile. "Teri," she called over her shoulder, "what are they saying?"

Teri had a baby in her arms, a young woman standing proudly beside her, and at least eight children clinging to her shirt and her legs. They all looked overjoyed to see Teri.

"They're probably asking your name," Teri said. "You can tell them that in English."

Jessica pointed to herself and said, "I'm Jessica."

The three little girls tried to pronounce Jessica but found it difficult.

"Jessica," she repeated. It didn't help. They couldn't say it.

The girls giggled and then pointed to themselves and rattled off their names, which Jessica found hard to understand and even harder to repeat. It didn't seem to matter to the little ones. They grasped Jessica's arms and pulled her over to where their mothers now stood, gathering with many of the other people from the small town.

It was a moving reception. The men shook hands heartily with Kyle and the other guys. The women slipped their rough, work-worn hands into Jessica's and warmly welcomed her. One older woman came up to Jessica, and speaking gently, she motioned for Jessica to bend down to her level so she could kiss Jessica on the cheek. Tears were in her eyes. Jessica wished she could understand what the woman was saying, even though in her heart the message was clear. These people were thrilled to see Kyle and his group. Jessica felt honored to be a part of them.

"Okay," Kyle said to the group after about twenty minutes of hugs and handshakes. "Let's put up these tents before it gets dark. Bill, can you and Joel start unloading the truck?"

Kyle stepped away from the group and came over to Jessica. He had a peculiar look on his face. It was that shy, little boy look mixed with a wrinkle of concern. "Jessica," he said quietly, "I need to talk to you for a minute. Alone."

Chapter Thirteen

*J*essica followed Kyle to the front of the van, away from everyone else. She couldn't believe the way her heart was pounding. What was wrong? Kyle looked so concerned.

Once they were away from the crowd, Kyle stood a respectable distance from Jessica and looked at his tennis shoes. It took him a moment before he looked up, and meeting her eyes, he said, "I feel really bad about something, and I want to clear things up before this weekend gets rolling."

Jessica felt uneasy. What was he about to say? That he wished she hadn't come on the trip? That she didn't belong here? That he was offended by the way she had treated him at her house several weeks ago? What?

"I have to be honest with you," Kyle said. "I feel a little uneasy around you. It's bothered me all day. Well, actually, it's bothered me for several weeks now. I don't know what upset you that day at your house…" Kyle waited for a response, but Jessica didn't say anything.

"And I don't exactly understand why you decided to come on this trip, when you knew I'd be here."

"Do you think I'm playing games with you?" Jessica asked defensively, and then wished she hadn't said anything.

Kyle placed his thumb and forefinger across his jaw, slowly rubbing his five o'clock shadow and then tapping his finger on his lips. Jessica had seen him make this gesture before. It seemed to signal that he was thinking before speaking.

"I think you're hiding something," Kyle said plainly. "I don't know what it is, and I guess it's none of my business. But, you see, I have this problem." He paused again. "My problem is that I find myself intensely attracted to you."

Jessica felt her throat tighten.

"But, you see, I don't know anything about you."

"Why are you telling me this?" Again Jessica heard herself saying the words before she thought them through.

"Because we're going to be together, working in rather close quarters these next few days, and as the sort of leader of this group, I need to ask you a few things. I've asked everyone who has come on this trip these questions. I should have asked you before we left. Better late than never, I guess," he said with half a shrug.

Jessica would not let herself become vulnerable. She would not give in, whatever it was Kyle asked her.

"I need to know where you stand spiritually," he said.

"Spiritually?"

Kyle nodded. "This is an outreach trip. It's not so much about helping the poor and needy as it is about telling them who Jesus is. That's why we've been building this church." He pointed to the half-finished structure in front of the van. "We started last year, but ran out of funds and materials. These people have been waiting a whole year for us to return and finish their church so they could have a place to worship. All the teens that came on this trip are believers. They've trusted Christ as their Savior and are eager to follow Him as the Lord of their lives."

Kyle looked at Jessica with his eyebrows slightly raised. She supposed he wanted her to fill in the pause with her convictions.

"I don't know where I stand, if that's what you're asking. I...." She stopped, trying to guard her words. "I don't know where I stand on a lot of things in my life right now. I guess you could say I'm on a journey."

Kyle's expression softened and so did his words. He nodded. "That's a good place to be. I want you to know that I consider myself to be on a journey, too. The one difference might be that eight years ago, I made a commitment to Jesus Christ. I surrendered my life to Him, and my journey is now directed by Him."

Jessica thought it was interesting that Dawn and Kyle had both said the same thing that day about surrendering to God and being committed to Christ. She hadn't known anyone in her life who had ever spoken in those terms. What did it mean? How were they any different than she?

"Kyle," one of the guys called from the back of the truck, "we need a lantern over here. It's too dark to see anything."

"I'll be right there," Kyle called back. Turning to Jessica, he grasped her arm, his large hand swallowing her elbow. "What I wanted to say is that I'm here for you, if you want me to be. And I wish that you would be open. That's all. Just be open." He gave her elbow a squeeze and then jogged off to help the guys.

Open? Open to what? Open to a relationship? He doesn't understand. It's not that easy.

Jessica slowly walked over to the group of girls, who were fumbling with a bunch of tent poles and squabbling over which end went in where. Kyle's phrase came back to her. "I find myself intensely attracted to you." *Why would he tell me that?*

"You can be in our tent," Dawn said to Jessica. "It's only Marjie and me. We have plenty of room." Jessica was glad to see that during the long van ride Dawn had managed to buddy up with one of the other girls. Jessica wasn't sure if she should come between them or if she should let them continue to develop their friendship without interference.

She ended up in Teri's tent, which was just big enough for the two of them. Jessica's sleeping bag had been a loan from Kyle, and as she rolled it out, it smelled of wood and campfires. Jessica zipped open her bag and pawed through her things in search of her bottle of saline solution and her lens case so she could take out her contacts.

"Where's the bathroom?" she asked Teri.

Teri pointed out the open flap of their tent with her powerful flashlight. It was now quite dark. The beam fell on a rough-hewn wooden outhouse. "There."

"Very funny," Jessica said. "I mean the real bathroom."

Teri started to laugh. "That's it!" She swirled her flashlight around in little loops, the light bouncing off the outhouse door. "*¡El Baño!*" Just then the door opened, and Bill stepped out, raising his arm to block Teri's flashlight from shining in his face.

"All right, I confess! Whatever it is, I confess!"

"Sorry," Teri called out, muffling her laugh.

Jessica leaned over and laughed into Teri's shoulder. "The poor guy!"

"Bill can handle it. He's a tough nut," Teri said.

"I'd certainly agree with the nut part," Jessica said.

"Hey, I heard that," Bill said, now standing a few feet away from their tent.

"No boys allowed in the girls' area," one of the girls from the tent next to Teri's called out, peeking through the front opening.

The teasing continued for another half hour as the group tried to settle into their tents and bed down for the night. It was only nine-thirty, but at their brief evening meeting Kyle had informed them that breakfast would be at six o'clock sharp, and everyone was expected to be there, dressed and ready to work on building the church.

Teri taught Jessica the fine art of washing with a baby wipe and brushing her teeth with a bottle of mouthwash instead of water. "I'll set the alarm for 5:15. Do you need more time than that?"

"For what?" Jessica asked. "Unless there's a hidden shower around here, why don't we sleep until 5:45. Fifteen minutes should be enough time to get ready before breakfast."

"You don't understand. We are the morning chefs. You and me, baby."

Jessica slipped into the sleeping bag and said, "I can see I should have asked a lot more questions before agreeing to come on this little outing. What else haven't you told me?"

"*Nada,*" Teri said innocently in Spanish. "Nothing."

"Yeah, right," Jessica said, snuggling down for the night. She had a backpack mat, also from Kyle, under her sleeping bag, which made it only slightly more comfortable. A dusty smell was all around her from the fine dirt that blew in through their open tent door. It was a warm night. Dry, dusty, and dirty. Not so far away they heard a dog snarling, followed by ferocious barking.

Teri popped out of her sleeping bag. "Maybe we better zip up this door. I'd rather be hot than become a mad dog's midnight snack."

Jessica lay quietly, listening to the fading sounds of a dog yipping in retreat. Lively, danceable music played on someone's radio in the distance, and the muffled voices and laughter of Kyle and a couple of the guys could be heard from their tent only a few yards away. Jessica strained to hear what they were saying. She only caught a few words here and there. Mostly Bill's. He was no doubt entertaining his tent mates.

Jessica slept fitfully that night, but Teri seemed to have no trouble dropping off right away. While Jessica listened to Teri's even breathing, she thought back on some of the things they had talked about on their drive down from San Diego. Teri had pointed out the turnoff on the freeway toward Escondido and talked about growing up in a large family with a father who was the pastor of a Spanish-speaking church. Teri had been to Mexico many times. She said she had only been to Nueva twice before and that Kyle's dream had been to build an orphanage here since this was one of the more prosperous villages in the valley. Many abandoned children were in the poorer surrounding villages, and they could be brought to an orphanage, if one existed.

Sleeping off and on, Jessica's dreams came to her with sporadic themes. Over and over a tape of Kyle's voice replayed his surprising statement, "I find myself intensely attracted to you." Then she dreamed of an orphanage filled with laughing Mexican children. She woke and thought of her father, then fell asleep again and dreamed of being back in her classroom. Charlotte Mendelson was walking in with a police officer at her side as Charlotte pointed her acrylic-nailed finger at Jessica. Waking with a start, Jessica listened to the silence, calming her emotions, and wondering what it would be like to talk to God openly, intimately the way Teri did. Why couldn't she do that?

Just when Jessica was ready to fall into a deep sleep, Teri's alarm went off right by her head, startling her into an upright position. Teri reached over, slapped off the alarm, turned on her flashlight, and sat up in her sleeping bag, reading something.

"What are you doing?" Jessica whispered.

"Reading my Bible," Teri answered. "Do you want me to read aloud?"

"No, that's okay. I need to make a trip to the lovely little outhouse." Jessica pulled on her jeans and tennis shoes and unzipped the tent. She was greeted by Bill's camera lens, right in her face.

"*¡Buenós dias, Senorita Fenton!* he said. *"¿Cómo estás?"*

"I'm going to como your estas in a minute," Jessica said, placing her hand in front of the camera.

"No photographs, please," Teri added in her best movie star voice.

"Hey, Bill, leave the women alone," Kyle called out from his tent.

"Best to let sleeping beauties lie, is that it?" Bill said with a predawn smile peering out from behind his video camera.

"Why don't you start up the camp stove and see if you can find the eggs." Kyle emerged from his tent just as a rooster came pecking its way across their camp, crowing his heart out.

"Cool," Bill said, "a Spanish-speaking rooster." He hoisted his camera back onto his shoulder, and slinking after the scrawny bird, he said, *"Hola,* Senor Rooster. Don't you want to be in the movies?"

Jessica made a quick trip to the outhouse and dove back into her tent. She was so tired she couldn't believe it. All she wanted to do was crawl into her sleeping bag and go back to sleep. But she wasn't going to get her wish. There was too much to do.

She tried her best to clean up with another wet towelette. Her contacts were a bit of a challenge, but she eventually succeeded in putting them in and joined Teri in the kitchen area of their camp, where Teri was stirring a big pan of scrambled eggs on the camp stove. Several of the girls were up, helping her with the paper plates, plastic glasses, and silverware. This was all new to Jessica. She had never been on a camping trip like this before and never had she seen a bunch of kids pitch in and appear to have so much fun working.

That's what Jessica noticed all day. These teens were having fun. It was hard work putting the roof on the church and finishing the interior. Several of the women from the village joined them in the morning along with the men who didn't have to work on Saturday. Dozens of children ran around, as did mangy dogs, scrawny cats, and a couple of chickens.

Jessica found the work tiring. She had never tried anything like this before and was amazed to find that she actually kind of liked it. The three little girls who had attached themselves to her last night found her and followed her around all morning. Whatever Jessica did, they wanted to do, which included hammering and painting.

Around noon, when they were all hot and exhausted, Teri went to work making sandwiches. Some of the guys found a spigot and in their best Spanish asked one of the Mexican women if they could use it to wash up. She agreed, and within minutes a water fight broke out. Even Jessica received a bucket full of water splashed across her back. She let out a shriek and spun around. Kyle stood a few feet away with an empty bucket in his hand and a grin on his face.

Jessica thought for a moment of how it would appear to the women of the village if she retaliated. Teri had instructed her on how to be sensitive to the culture since the women in the village tended to be more reserved and modest than American women. Quickly glancing around, she noticed that all the women and most of the children had gone home for their mid-day meal and perhaps a siesta. The only ones watching were the teens from their group, and they all seemed eager to see how Jessica would react.

"Thanks," she said to Kyle with a smile. "I was getting a little too hot."

"*De nada,*" Kyle said in Spanish. "You're welcome. Any time." He sauntered off with the other guys, back to their beach chairs on the other side of the truck where Teri was passing out sandwiches.

Jessica retreated to her tent and grabbed her plastic sports bottle, which had been free with a drink she had bought yesterday. She carried it back to the camp kitchen. When no one was looking, she popped the stopper on the ice chest and filled her sports bottle with icy water. Then she walked over to join the lunch bunch.

Kyle had his back to her and was stuffing a large bite of his peanut butter and jelly sandwich into his mouth. No one seemed to notice her approach since Bill was busy entertaining them by making his sandwich into a talking puppet while Joel videotaped him. Jessica slipped in behind Kyle, opened the lid, and poured the icy water down his back.

"Yeow!" Kyle hollered, jumping out of his seat and spinning to face his opponent. He looked shocked and a bit delighted to discover it was Jessica. She smiled and strutted over to the card table to pick up her lunch plate.

"I got Kyle's reaction on tape!" Joel said triumphantly. "You're the first one on record who has been able to pay him back. Every year he gets us, but somehow we can't quite get him."

"It's because I sleep with my eyes open," Kyle said, giving a slight, involuntary shiver and sitting back in his beach chair. "Good thing I'm not the vengeful type, Senorita Morgan!"

Morgan! Everything seemed to stop for Jessica. She caught Kyle's gaze and searched it frantically. What else did he know about her?

"You mean, Senorita Fenton," Bill corrected him.

"Right. Senorita Fenton," Kyle said. His look at Jessica was one of compassion, one that said, "Come on, you can trust me."

But did she dare?

Chapter Fourteen

*A*ll afternoon Jessica worked alongside the teens and many eager village children. Mentally she processed every angle on how Kyle could know her real last name. He could have checked her wallet when he had her purse. Ida could have told him when he picked up the key to the house. Perhaps he had noticed the luggage tag the day she moved in. Or Charlotte could have tried to use her information to turn him against Jessica. Of all the options, Ida telling him was the most comforting. It would account for his reaction the afternoon he told her that secrets only become heavier the longer you carry them around.

Jessica tried to decide if his knowing her name had changed anything. Did it mean she could let down her guard and tell Kyle what she was running from? No, that was out of the question. All it meant was that he had a bit of information about her she wished he didn't have. But it didn't change anything.

At least none of her students seemed to think of it as anything more than an odd mix-up. That is, all but Dawn.

Toward the end of the afternoon she helped Jessica wash out paint brushes. Dawn had white paint in her hair and on her overalls, and even a few flecks had been sprinkled in her eyebrows. But Jessica had observed how much fun Dawn had acquiring each spot.

"Why did Kyle call you Señorita Morgan?" Dawn asked, looking down at the brushes in the bucket of milky water.

"Who knows?" Jessica said lightly. "Do you want to help me with dinner? Teri went to visit one of the women down the road, and I could use some help."

"Okay," Dawn said.

Jessica snuck a couple of quick peeks at Dawn out of the corner of her eye. Was it her imagination, or was Dawn looking at her differently?

I'm becoming neurotic!

Jessica put on a smile for Dawn. "Come on, let's get started. Teri told me she would leave everything out."

Jessica and Dawn washed up in a bucket of clear water and found Teri's dinner fixings on the folding table. Spaghetti. Easy enough. They filled a big pot with pure water and tossed in the spaghetti noodles. Dawn opened the jumbo can of sauce, and Jessica found two loaves of prepared garlic bread. They had to hunt through the trunk of Kyle's camping gear to find another pot for the sauce.

"I have to tell you," Jessica said to Dawn once their endeavor was well underway, "I don't cook much. My specialties are Marie Callender's frozen microwave dinners." She swatted at a few pesky flies and noticed how it was finally beginning to cool off.

Dawn laughed. "That's all I know how to make, too. Sometimes I cook scrambled eggs. Oh, and I have made chocolate chip cookies a few times. It's funny because you should see our kitchen. It's huge, with all these fancy machines like a pasta maker and a food processor. The joke is, we never use them. My dad and I buy frozen dinners or eat out."

"That is kind of ironic, isn't it?" Jessica said.

"I think the weird part is that I remember going to my grandma's house for dinner when I was little, and she had this tiny kitchen—no dishwasher, no garbage disposal—and I think she had like three pots and one frying pan. She used to make these great meals. She was an awesome cook. And she never owned a microwave or a food processor in her life."

Jessica laughed and then went hunting until she found a big wooden spoon to stir the sauce. "I can't say that I've ever prepared anything for fifteen people before, either."

"Sixteen," Dawn corrected her, batting the flock of tiny mosquitoes away from her face. "Fifteen people were coming on this trip, and then you made sixteen. I'm really glad you came."

"I think I am, too. It's so different down here, isn't it? The people and their way of life. It makes a person do some reflecting." Out of the corner of her eye, Jessica noticed something over her shoulder. It was Bill's camera.

"And here, folks, we have one of our famous mystery meals," Bill said as he zoomed in on the bubbling pot of red sauce.

"It's only spaghetti," Dawn said.

"Yeah, that's what they all say. The question is, what's in the sauce?"

"Lizard bellies, gopher guts, and rotten bee brains," Kyle said, stepping into their conversation.

"You're not too far off in your prediction," Jessica said, swatting at another fly. She shook her head at the same time, hoping to discourage the mosquito hoard which suddenly showed up, acting as if Jessica's ears were on their dinner menu. "Where did all these bugs come from?"

"They sleep during the heat of the day and come out when it cools off," Kyle said.

"Great," Dawn said. "Which do you prefer? Heat or bugs?"

"Yes, ladies and gentlegerms, that *is* the question tonight. Which do *you* prefer? Heat or bugs? Call in now. Our operators are standing by to record your response." Bill kept talking to himself as he walked toward the girls' tents, with one eye closed and the other squinting through his camera.

"Does anybody else worry about that guy?" Jessica asked.

"He's one of a kind," Kyle said. "I think he's going to be a game show host when he grows up."

Kyle came up behind Jessica, leaned over her shoulder, and looked in the pot of sauce. "How's dinner coming?"

Jessica thought about how she and Kyle, even in the midst of this dirty, primitive setting, could pretend they were in a cozy kitchen of their own. She could lift the wooden spoon up for him to taste the sauce while cupping her hand underneath it to catch any drips. Or she could say, "Go wash up, dear. I'll light the dinner candles, and you can pour the champagne." These scenes were all from black-and-white reruns she had watched on Nick at Nite. Images—strong images—in her mind of what a family should be.

Jessica didn't move. She knew that, if she turned around to look at Kyle, his face would be only inches from hers. "We're getting there," she said flatly and then, as Kyle walked away, she drew in a deep breath. She wanted to hold on to that scent of freshly washed skin that Kyle took with him. It was the smell of earth, sweat, and flesh rinsed with Ivory soap. The clean fragrance splashed up first, but in its wake lingered the manly, deeper scent that is earned only by hard work. She had known few men who carried that scent.

"Whoa!" Dawn squawked. The pot of spaghetti noodles had begun to boil over, its white, bubbly starch lava forging a path down the side of the silver pot. "How do you turn this thing off?"

Jessica fiddled with all the knobs on the side until both the burners went out with a puff. "I'd say dinner is ready. Come and get it, you guys!"

"Or should we say, come and regret it." Bill ventured over with his camera on his shoulder and the gang behind him. "Our cooks tonight do not provide any warranties with the meal, folks. Dine at your own risk."

That night, once everyone had settled into their tents, Jessica lingered outside, sitting alone on the ice chest. She gazed up at the velvet sky, flecked with iridescent stars, and thought about what she should wish for. She wanted something. She could feel it deep inside. Not something. It was someone.

I wish for Kyle.

But she had Kyle. Or rather, with very little effort she could have Kyle. He had made it clear he was interested in her. But that wasn't it. Her longing was deeper than that. She had felt this ache many times. In the past, she had called it loneliness. Lately, she thought the ache was part of her mourning over her mother. Tonight it seemed different. When placed up against the experiences she had had these past few days, her longing seemed more intense than ever. Something was not right in her life. Something had been taken from her. And she wanted it back.

From over in the tent area, a zipper ran down its track. In the shadows, Jessica could just make out Teri's frame stepping out of their tent. She approached Jessica with her flashlight shining a path ahead of her.

"There you are," Teri said when the light came upon Jessica. "Are you okay?"

"I'm fine. Just thinking."

Teri looked up at the sky. "Wow! Look at all the stars tonight. Did you know that one of those stars was lit for me?"

"Oh, did you send in for that science promotion at school where you pay to have them name the next discovered star after you?" Jessica said.

"No," Teri said. "I'm talking about a promise God made to Abraham, the patriarch of the Hebrew nation."

"Right," Jessica said, not having any idea where Teri could possibly be going with this. "I know who Abraham is."

"God promised Abraham that his descendants would be as many as the stars in the heavens and as many as the grains of sand on the sea."

"Are you telling me that you're actually from a Jewish heritage?" Jessica asked.

"No, no, nothing like that. I'm a believer, a follower of Christ. I'm one of the ones who will receive the blessing of God, the inheritance promised to Abraham. Only I receive it through adoption. I'm not a slave under the law but a daughter, a daughter of the King of this universe."

Jessica squinted in the darkness, trying to see Teri's face. "Teresa Moreno, I have absolutely no idea what you are talking about. Are we on line with the same conversation here?"

"I'm sorry," Teri said. "It comes from being a pastor's kid. I grew up with all the Bible lingo, so it seems natural to me. What I'm trying to say is that I know I have eternal life. That's all."

Jessica laughed. "That's all? That's a pretty bold declaration. I've met people three times your age who have searched all their lives and can't make that claim."

"They must not know Jesus," Teri said. "He's the only way. They simply haven't been restored—cleansed from their sins and brought back into a right relationship with God."

"Yeah, well, I guess we all need a right relationship with God," Jessica said, trying to make this a win-win conversation. "And I guess what you and I need most right now is some sleep." Jessica rose and began to walk back to their tent.

"Can I say something to you?" Teri asked, hurrying to catch up with Jessica's long strides.

"I don't know," Jessica said, feeling all her defenses rise. "Can you?"

"I'm not very good at saying this the right way," Teri began. They were now in front of their tent and had stopped before going inside. Teri was speaking softly, yet Jessica wondered if the people in the other tents, particularly Kyle, could hear her. "What I want to say is that maybe it's time you stopped running away, Jessica. I want you to know God."

"Well, that certainly is saying it," Jessica said, bending over to untie her tennis shoes. She took off her dusty shoes and left them outside the tent. Then, unzipping the door, she crawled in first with Teri right behind her.

"That's all I'll say about it," Teri said once they were in their sleeping bags and the flashlight was turned out. "I really care about you, Jess. I don't want you to go to hell."

The night was silent except for the distant barking of a dog.

Teri let out a heavy sigh. "That didn't come out the way I wanted it to. I've never been good at witnessing."

"I think we should just get some sleep," Jessica said.

A thin hush wavered in the air between them.

"I'm sorry," Teri whispered. "I didn't mean to sound so abrupt. Please try to hear my heart and not my clumsy words."

"Don't worry about it," Jessica said.

"Good night," Teri said softly.

"Good night." Jessica was already drifting off as she said the words. She slept until the emaciated rooster decided to use the front mat of their tent as its platform to announce the new day.

"Get out of here!" Jessica yelled, tossing her pillow at the tent door. "What time is it?"

Teri held the travel alarm close to her face and said, "It's 5:27. Stupid *gallo!*" she yelled at the rooster.

Jessica rolled over and groaned. "I am so stiff. I don't think I can move. Why are my arms so sore?"

"All that painting," Teri suggested. "My neck hurts. Maybe we'll feel better if we get up and stretch."

Jessica didn't feel better stretching. She didn't feel better after eating, either. When the group gathered in its circle of beach chairs, she sat slouched in her low chair and wrapped her work shirt around her like a blanket. The sky was overcast, a severe contrast to the heat they had battled the day before. It felt like rain.

"We need to get right to work," Kyle said, keeping an eye on the darkening sky. "My guess is that the roof will take us about two more hours, and we want to seal it before these clouds deliver their goods. You guys remember that first year when it rained for two days straight right before we arrived?"

"I do," Bill said. "The roads around here turn into giant mud wrestling pits."

"Could make for some interesting filming," Joel suggested, tossing his paper plate in the trash bag. A few relentless bees were buzzing around the opening of the bag. "Where is your camera, anyway?"

"It better be in the tent," Bill said. "Not that I don't trust all the people in this one-pig town, but I don't." He hopped up and went over to his tent. A moment later he emerged victoriously holding up his camera.

"Oh, great," Brenda, one of the girls, groaned. "Another day with Wild Bill on his imaginary movie set. Do you think reality will ever set in with that guy?"

"I hope not," Teri said. "He's too fun the way he is."

"Yes, well, try going out with him," Brenda said confiden-tially. "It's real funny for the first hour or so. Then you want to be serious, and he doesn't switch over." She had short black hair cut in a bob. Her dark eyebrows framed tender gray eyes under eyelashes that would never need the touch of a mascara wand.

"Bill can be serious," Teri said.

"I've never seen it," Brenda retorted.

"I get the feeling you would like him to be a little more seri-ous about you. Am I right?"

Brenda blushed. "Is it that obvious?"

"No, not to normal people," Teri said with a comforting smile. "But you see, I'm not normal. I have this bizarre gift of spotting these things a mile away. Come help me clean up the breakfast mess."

Jessica could hear Teri giving Brenda her advice on guys as they walked arm and arm into the kitchen area. When Teri had something to say, she sure said it.

The rest of the group had already tossed the breakfast dishes and set about the task of finishing the roof on the church. Jessica still didn't feel well. All she wanted was a nice hot bath. A lukewarm shower, even. Her hair was pulled back in a ponytail, to keep it out of her face. Dawn had volunteered to braid Jessica's hair while Jessica was trying to eat her break-fast, but she didn't feel like having anyone touch her. Not even her hair. She realized she was the only one left in the "dining room," as they had dubbed it, and was about to uncurl from her huddled position and stand up when she felt a pair of strong hands firmly grasp her shoulders.

"Sore?" Kyle asked.

"Miserably sore," Jessica answered, allowing herself to relax as Kyle rubbed her shoulders. It felt so good. Her hands started to tingle from the improved circulation, and her headache started to ease up. Suddenly Kyle stopped and took his hands off of her.

"*Buenos días,* Hermano Cristobal," Kyle greeted a man dressed in a white shirt and dark slacks coming toward them. Jessica stayed in her seat as the two men shook hands and spoke to each other in Spanish. When they finished, the man nodded at Jessica without making direct eye contact. It was a polite way of acknowledging her presence. Kyle shook hands with Cristobal again, and then the man left. Returning to Jessica, Kyle scratched his neck and said, "That was kind of awkward."

"What? Did he ask you for something?"

"No, I mean his seeing me touch you was awkward. It's not acceptable in their culture, especially among the Christians, for a man to touch a woman like that."

"Like what? You were only rubbing my shoulders, which I appreciated very much. Nothing is sinful about that. Right?"

"Not in our minds maybe. Their culture is different." Kyle looked embarrassed. "Cristobal is going to deliver a dedication message at the church tonight. I would never want to do anything to offend him."

Jessica thought Kyle had a lot of integrity to be so concerned about offending the man. And she did understand the importance of honoring cultural differences.

"Don't worry about it," Jessica said lightly. "I appreciated the back rub. If you knew how badly I needed it, you would realize that getting me out of this chair and up and going today is probably much more important than what that man thought."

"You're really hurting, huh?"

"This is all new for me. I haven't even been camping before. Not really. Not like this."

"Then I'm impressed," Kyle said. From his abundance of

camping gear, he obviously was a seasoned pro at living in the outdoors.

Their eyes met. Locked. Jessica could feel her heart being lured out of its wintry isolation and drawn to the warmth she saw in his gaze. She emotionally took one tiny step toward Kyle. He seemed to stand ready, waiting for her to make the next move. Suddenly something inside her turned cold, and she ran behind the cement wall of her lonely soul once more.

"I guess I better get to work on the roof," Jessica said, her words falling over each other like tumbling dominoes. "Especially if you're right about the rain. I'll find a couple of aspirin and be right there." She walked off toward her tent. Behind her she could feel Kyle's gaze. He hadn't moved. Once again Jessica realized that she was the one who was running away.

Chapter Fifteen

"What do you think?" Bill asked Jessica as she stood in front of the church and scanned the roof where ten or so students were busy about their tasks.

"What do I think of the church? I think it's coming along nicely."

"I think," Bill began, then stopped and picked up his camera, handed it to Jessica, and said, "get this on film. This is profound."

Jessica adjusted the lens to her eye and pushed the "on" button.

"I think," Bill said, stretching out his hand toward the church, "that the house that is a-building looks not as the house that is built."

Jessica pulled the camera down and gave Bill a big smile. "So you did learn something in my class!"

Bill looked proud of himself. "Wait till you see this place

tonight. It will look completely different when it fills up with people."

Bill's prediction came true. It looked completely different, all right—because it was pouring rain. It had rained continually since around two that afternoon. They had managed to finish the roof and make lunch before the rain came. Kyle spoke with Cristobal, and they decided to hold the dedication service at five instead of seven since the rain didn't seem to have any inclination to let up.

Kyle then decided they should pack up that afternoon instead of staying one more night in their tents. They would leave the village right after the service and drive back to Calexico where they would find a cheap hotel. No one complained about the possibility of hot showers that night. In record time the group packed up their tents and tossed all the soggy gear into the back of the truck. Everything was a muddy mess.

Teri, Kyle, and several of the students made raincoats out of plastic trash bags and slogged through the village inviting the people to come at five. Jessica stayed inside the church with two girls and tried to sweep out the construction dust and stray nails littering the cement floor.

In the midst of their cleaning, the church door opened. Seven children, three women, and two men entered, completely drenched. They greeted Jessica and the girls with warm handshakes. Then the women sat on the wooden benches on one side of the church, and the two men stood by the back door.

Jessica checked her watch. It was only 4:20. These people were early, and they weren't alone. More people started coming in. Each of them shook hands, greeting Jessica and the teens. By 4:45 the church was filled. Outside, the rain continued.

"What should we do?" Jessica asked the girls. "Our only

two interpreters are gone, and these people seem ready to start the meeting. Do either of you speak Spanish?"

The students shook their heads. "I brought some sock puppets," one of the girls said. "Maybe we could do a little show or something."

Before they had a chance to work out the details, the church door opened again, and two teenage boys from the village let a squealing pig loose inside. It ran around, wildly snorting and squealing and leaving muddy streaks across the cement floor. The children loved it. The women were horrified. The men cornered the bewildered animal and corralled it back out the front door. Just as the pig went squealing on its way, Kyle and Teri arrived with the rest of the group. Another thirty or so people came with them.

Bill was right. The church that was a-building was nothing like the church that was built. Jessica didn't know how they managed to pack so many people into the small building. She was grateful that she had found a place to sit early on. One of her little friends perched on her lap, and the other two sat at Jessica's feet. The smell of their wet hair and clothes was almost overpowering. Although it wasn't just them. Everyone smelled moldy. Teri managed to wedge in next to Jessica on the bench and scooped up two little girls onto her lap.

At exactly five o'clock, Cristobal and Kyle stepped to the front of the room and onto the small platform Kyle had built. Kyle looked as if he were about to burst with joy. Cristobal spoke first. Jessica could figure out that he welcomed everyone and then asked them to stand.

"Vamos a orar," Cristobal said, lifting his Bible over his head and closing his eyes.

"Pray," Teri whispered to Jessica. Jessica closed her eyes and heard a slow rumbling across the room as men and women agreed with Cristobal's prayer, which he spoke in bold, sincere tones. The praying sounded like a brook running to meet the ocean, getting louder as it became wider.

"Amen, amen," Cristobal concluded, and everyone in the room echoed, "Amen, amen." Jessica remembered hearing the teens say the same thing when they were at their final meeting. This must be where they had picked it up.

The group sat down, and Teri, taking her girls back onto her lap, leaned over to Jessica and whispered, "He holds the Bible over his head like that to show he wants to be under God's authority." Teri continued to interpret for Jessica in hushed words as the service went on.

Kyle spoke for a few minutes. His Spanish seemed fluent enough, but his words were halting, and Jessica thought she saw tears in his eyes. She realized that for Kyle, seeing his dream come true, had to be rewarding. Perhaps one day he would stand on another platform in this village and dedicate his orphanage.

Then the music began. Cristobal took up a guitar, and two young men joined him, both with guitars as well. Without song books or any words provided, the people began to sing. Their singing touched something deep inside Jessica, and she longed to join in. She looked at Teri. Teri's eyes were closed, her face tilted upward, and tears were streaming down her cheeks as she sang her heart out.

Outside the rain poured down, and inside the people sang on. Never had Jessica felt so moved.

Just look at how captivated these people are with worshipping God.

For the next hour several men spoke, each of them talking about how God had provided for them. Jessica thought their speeches were small, yet their faith and trust were large. Her trust was small. As Teri interpreted, Jessica listened to one of the men say that since the day he came to know Christ, three years ago, he had found that God provided everything he needed. Not everything he wanted, but everything he needed.

It made Jessica think of her zucchini and the groceries and even the DoveBars. What a silly thing to connect God with. Yet to her it was the first evidence she had seen that God was merciful and caring and that he desired to "bless" her, as Teri would say. She knew then that either she had to believe God was a personal God who cared about her, or she had to reject God altogether. She couldn't remain distant from him or run away. Not tonight. Not here, in the midst of all these people.

More messages, more prayers, and more singing followed. At the end, Kyle prayed. He also held a Bible over his head and ended with "Amen, Amen."

The official dedication of the church was over, but the hugging and good-byes went on for another hour. Children ran wild in the suffocating little room. Dozens of young women tried to start up conversations with Jessica. She had to regretfully shake her head and offer them a little hug instead of conversation.

Teri had her hands full interpreting for everyone as well as exchanging a final few words with some of the women she seemed close to. One of the young women, Letty, had helped all weekend on the church and seemed enthusiastic and encouraging to the teens. Jessica noticed Dawn standing beside Letty, their arms around each other while Bill captured their smiling faces with his video camera. Dawn had blossomed during the weekend, not only in relating to the Mexican women and children, but also in fitting in with the youth group.

Dawn really didn't need me to come. I'm glad I did, though.

Jessica's opinion quickly changed when they left the shelter of the building and made a dash for the van. It was still raining. All the wet and mud made Jessica hang back, waiting until the last minute. She noticed Kyle delivering to Cristobal the boxes of clothes and supplies the church had sent down with them.

"Come on," Teri called, lifting her trash bag up with both arms. "We can both fit under here."

Jessica slid in next to Teri, and four little children joined them, like baby ducks hiding under their mother's wide, down girth. They took about four nimble steps in the mud; then Teri slipped and fell down face first, pulling her canopy and two of the children with her.

"Are you okay?" Jessica bent down and tried to help Teri up.

Teri was laughing so hard she couldn't answer. She was black across the front, all mud except for the whites of her eyes and teeth. "What a klutz!" she chided herself. Teri rose and checked on the little ones, who were also laughing. "I hope my suitcase is near the back of the truck," she said, wiping the glops of mud from her cheeks. "I don't think the border guards would let me out of the country looking like this." Teri took a step and nearly fell again. "Ouch!" She grabbed her right leg and tried to hop quickly on the other foot. "My ankle," she said.

Jessica offered Teri her arm, and they hobbled over to the van where a dozen teens were watching the comedy routine, none of them aware that Teri was hurt. Bill's camera was rolling from the open side door of the van, his running commentary keeping the crowd laughing.

"You guys, she's really hurt," Jessica yelled.

"I'm okay," Teri said.

"No you're not. You can't even walk."

"Kyle," Bill called out, putting down the camera and trying to capture Kyle's attention. "Kyle, over here. Teri's hurt!"

Teri sat down on the step inside the van door and caught her breath. Jessica stood next to her, the rain coursing down her back, and the mud from Teri dripping off her arm. Kyle sprinted over, picking his way through the mud. The minute he saw Teri's mud covered face, he burst out laughing. "This is the best joke you've pulled all week! Was this Bill's idea?"

"Kyle, she hurt her ankle," Jessica said.

His smile disappeared. "Which one is it, Teri?" Jessica recognized the rescuer tone in his voice.

It took nearly an hour, even with the help of the people there, to get Teri cleaned up, changed, and her ankle wrapped. Jessica and some of the soaked teens took advantage of the opportunity to change into drier clothes too.

The only good thing about the delay was that the rain let up. After another round of tears, hugs, and good-byes, Kyle pulled Jessica off to the side, out of sight from the rest of the group. They stood behind the church, their feet sinking into the soft, clay mud.

"I don't think Teri should drive," Kyle said.

Jessica swallowed hard. "So you want me to drive the truck?"

Kyle looked at her without answering. His green eyes scanned hers in search of a willing spirit.

Jessica looked away. "I guess it's the only logical solution. I follow you, right?"

Kyle nodded. He reached for her elbow and gave it a tender squeeze. "Thanks, Jess." He had never called her that before. She loved the way it sounded, rolling out of that deep chest and falling softly on her heart. "You're a lifesaver."

"I thought that was your occupation," Jessica said quickly. A crooked grin pulled at the corner of her mouth, and she felt the familiar, ever so slight tug of her half-moon scar.

Kyle's hand moved toward her, and before she realized what he was doing, he touched her tiny scar, tenderly tracing the half-circle with his large, rough finger. Jessica reached up and clasped his hand, drawing his palm to her cheek. She closed her eyes and felt Kyle's open hand cupping her chin and cheek. Kyle did not pull away. Jessica did not move.

All Jessica could think of were Kyle's words from the first night in the village: *"I'm here for you, if you want me to be. I wish that you would be open. That's all. Just be open."* Right now Jessica felt as if her heart were more open than it had been in months—no, in years. It seemed crazy to feel that way while standing in a mud puddle in Mexico.

"Kyle," Jessica whispered, opening her eyes and looking up at him. No other words followed. All that emerged was a tiny tear that skittered down her cheek.

He smiled. "I see it's beginning to heal nicely." He traced the half-moon again before withdrawing his hand.

"I hope so," Jessica said, feeling herself blush. She felt as if something inside her was healing as well.

Suddenly she felt self-conscious. She looked away and asked, "Do you want Teri to ride with me in the truck?"

"Oh, um," Kyle cleared his throat. "Actually, I fixed a place for Teri in the van so she could keep her foot elevated. Have you seen inside the cab of the truck? We packed everything in such a hurry we had to put some of the sleeping bags in the front seat with you. No else could fit in there."

Jessica tried to appear calm.

"Here are the keys." Kyle pulled them from his pocket and handed them to Jessica. "Are you going to be all right driving by yourself? We could move some of the junk into the van and put someone else in there with you."

It began to sprinkle, and Jessica thought of how long they already had been delayed. "No, I'm sure I'll be fine. Just don't leave me in the dust. Or, should I say, in the mud."

"It won't be hard to keep an eye on you. One of the front headlights broke since we've been here. It'll make it easier for me to watch for you, but I'm sure it'll make it harder for you to see the road. Be careful, okay? And if you want me to stop for any reason, just blink your brights a few times, and I'll pull over."

"Okay," Jessica agreed. She took the keys and sloshed to the truck, determined to prove she was a rugged woman who could conquer any situation, even a muddy, remote Mexican road at night in the middle of a rainstorm. She was strong and independent. She could do this.

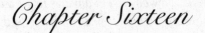

Chapter Sixteen

The windshield wipers on the truck fiercely beat back and forth, clearing Jessica's view. The van rolled down the paved road several comfortable yards in front of her. Its red taillights were the only illumination she could see in the blackness of the stormy night. Kyle was right about it being hard to see the road with only one headlight. Driving out of the village was tricky and so was coercing the truck to cooperate in the mud. When the tires connected with the firm asphalt on the main road, Jessica breathed a little easier.

She didn't see the first pothole before she hit it, but when she did, the jolt jarred her teeth and caused her hands to grip the steering wheel in fear. She remembered only too well how quickly her last accident had happened. Tonight all the elements were against her, and she could almost feel the impending threat of an accident if she made one imprecise move. Slowing down, Jessica scanned the road ahead of her, trying to assess every bump or curve before she came to it.

Come on, Kyle, slow down! I'm anxious to get out of here, too, but you don't have to drive fifty miles an hour on this death trap road.

The rain let up, and Jessica allowed herself to ease her grip on the steering wheel. Her neck began to ache. She stretched her shoulders and remembered how wonderful Kyle's short back rub had felt yesterday.

Her imagination carried her off to some illusory world where she lived without any complicated secrets. In that world, she easily fell into Kyle's embrace. She eagerly trusted him with her heart, her lips, her self.

Bright lights shone in her side mirror, momentarily blinding Jessica and bringing her out of the fantasy realm and back to the real, cold, wet world. The truck behind her barreled right up on her bumper, shining its headlights at her relentlessly.

"Go around me, buddy," she muttered. "Get off my tail!"

The rattletrap truck pulled out and around Jessica, then slowed down in front of her, wedging a greater distance between her and the van.

"Now go around the van, you crazy driver!"

But the truck didn't obey her commands. The driver seemed pleased to slow down to a rather comfortable pace of thirty-five miles an hour and visually block her off from Kyle. Now it was Jessica's turn to flash her brights, not only at the stubborn truck in front of her, but also with the hope that Kyle would see and pull over as he had promised. The truck ahead of her didn't respond.

Even though she couldn't see the van, she noticed there were virtually no turnouts along the road. Kyle was unlikely to turn off this main road.

For several miles Jessica followed close behind the belligerent truck, occasionally catching a whiff of its rancid petroleum fumes. She tried to pass the truck a couple of times. But she always changed her mind at the last minute, not willing to risk it with only one headlight and a pitch black road ahead of her filled with unseen potholes. After a while, Jessica gave up and fell into line behind the truck. She concluded that he must be going to the border as well, and she would reconnect with Kyle when he could pull the van off to the side.

Then another pair of headlights shone in her mirror. This car didn't seem to want to go around her; rather, it seemed content to sit on her tail and drive with its high beams on. Jessica adjusted her posture so the bright lights wouldn't hit right in her eyes. For the next twenty minutes Jessica drove with both eyes on the road immediately in front of her, dodging holes, and trying not to let the windshield wipers hypnotize her.

All of a sudden the truck in front veered to the right. Jessica followed it and drove a short distance before realizing that the truck had left the main road. The road they were on had turned into bumpy gravel. Jessica came to a stop. Nothing was around her in the darkness but soybean fields. She inched the truck forward, looking for another gravel road or a place wide enough to turn around. The rattling old truck she had followed was long gone, and no cars, homes, or lights of any kind were visible for as far as she could see.

"Okay," she coached herself. "Just turn around and go back. Find a wide enough spot. Over here! This looks promising."

Jessica slowly made a loop in the gravel and edged the front tires onto the muddy bean field. "Slow and steady now. Keep going, keep going. Don't stop—"

Too late. When the back tires hit the mud, they lost all traction and spun wildly as Jessica frantically revved the engine. Her front right tire and both back tires appeared to be in the mud. Only the front left tire remained on the gravel road. Now she was scared. The rain was pelting against the windshield like mushy peas, and it felt as if the back of the truck was sinking rapidly into the soft earth.

Jessica sat for several minutes, trying not to panic. All around her outside was nothing but liquid blackness. She checked both doors to make sure they were locked. Certainly Kyle saw her turn off. He would be here any minute, and the van could pull her out of the mud. She would tell him to drive slower the rest of the way so she could keep up with him. And he would squeeze her elbow or touch her cheek again and tell her he was sorry. Jessica had it all worked out in her mind. She sat alone with her "Kyle to the rescue" scenario to keep her company.

She waited. The rain splattered against her windshield. The truck slowly tilted to the right as it inched its way deeper into the mud. An hour passed and Kyle never came.

Now she was mad. *Why did he have to drive so fast? Why did that stupid truck cut me off? How did I miss the road? Why is this happening to me, God? Don't you care about what happens to me? Is this your idea of a good time—watching me sweat like this? I don't think it's very funny.*

Jessica realized she was talking to God as if he could hear her. True, she was yelling at him in her head, but she was addressing him differently than she ever had before. After being around these "believers," as Teri called them, and sitting through the evening's church service, Jessica's opinion of God was beginning to change.

"Okay," she said aloud, attempting to pray. "You've got me cornered, God. You have my full attention. What do you want?"

For some reason, the image that came to mind was of Kyle and Cristobal holding their Bibles over their heads when they prayed. What was it Teri had said? To show they were under God's authority.

That concept hit at Jessica's core. She refused to put herself under anyone's authority. Her philosophy of life centered around being in control of herself, her circumstances, and the way she allowed other people to treat her. Yet, in the solitude of this very dark night, she had control over nothing.

Jessica felt weak, utterly at a loss as to how to hold together the frayed threads of her life. She felt that intense longing well up inside her, that yearning for someone, that passion to be restored, reunited. Only now, for the first time, she realized she wasn't longing for her mother. Or for Kyle or any other human. She thirsted for God.

The realization disturbed her. To somehow be connected with God, to be under his control and authority, to surrender—it wasn't "her." But it was what she longed for. It struck her as a strange bargain. Her life, failures and all, in exchange for God's favor.

"But you're so perfect," she argued aloud with God. "You have everything. Why would you want me?" She knew the answer. She had known it since she left L.A. Even if a father has absolutely everything, he still wants to be on harmonious terms with his daughter. Before Jessica realized what she was doing, she began to cry. "I'm sorry," she whispered into the unseen ear of her heavenly Father. "I'm sorry. Forgive me. If you really want me, you can have me. I want to know you. I surrender." She sobbed softly and whispered again, "I surrender to you, God."

Jessica heard the sound of a car engine coming down the road. *I'm saved!* she thought jubilantly, peering into the darkness. But only darkness was in front of the truck. Then she caught a glimmer of a headlight in the side mirror, and she froze.

That can't be Kyle. He would come from the other direction. What if it's… She didn't want to think of the possibilities. A deserted road in the middle of the night was no place for a woman to be under the best of circumstances. Sitting alone in a disabled truck in the middle of Mexico was the worst she could imagine.

The vehicle stopped behind her. She could hear loud men's voices as they approached the truck. One of them laughed the clumsy guffaw of a drunkard.

Jessica knew the doors were locked. Still, she felt like a sitting duck. The men stopped at the back of the U-Haul and tried the door. It rattled but didn't open. She knew they would be coming to the front any second now! With no time to lose, Jessica slid to the floor on the passenger side of the truck and covered herself with the pile of sleeping bags from the seat. She lay frozen in one position, barely allowing herself to breathe. Terrified, she listened in the darkness. Someone tried the door handle on the driver's side, found it locked and kept rattling it. Someone else did the same on the passenger's side. Jessica felt as if her heart would beat right out of her chest and knock the sleeping bags off the top of her. She imagined the men looking inside, trying to decide if it was worth the effort to break the window.

Just then one of them called from the back of the truck. With her back pressed against the floor, Jessica could feel the vibration of the back door being rolled open, exposing all their luggage and Kyle's expensive camping gear. The men by the front windows abandoned their quest and joined the others at the back of the truck. From the hoots and hollers, Jessica could picture them looting the back of the truck, taking as much as they could as fast as they could.

She stayed frozen in her twisted position on the floor, praying they wouldn't break open the front windows and steal her camouflage. Then she heard it, the sound of their vehicle's motor starting up and rumbling past her down the dirt road.

Jessica swallowed great gulps of air trying to calm down and convince herself she was now safe. They were gone.

For the next five minutes or so, she remained paralyzed in her hiding place, not daring to pop up her head. She imagined a twisted face pressed against the window staring in at her. Not one of Bill's "squashed bug" imitation faces, but a man's drunken face.

Oh, God! Where are you? Save me! Protect me!

An inexplicable peace began to come over Jessica. Her heart rate returned to normal, and she felt almost comfortable, tucked in her little hiding place. It occurred to her that she was indeed safe. Nothing had happened to her. God had protected her. It made her think of some of the other "coincidences" that had occurred in the past few weeks: Kyle being there when the accident happened; the zucchini from her garden; the groceries on her doorstep, with DoveBars included. And now, the covering of the sleeping bags that had been tossed into the front seat so haphazardly.

Before this trip Jessica might have written those circumstances off as "fate." Now she felt differently. In these past few days, God had become real to her, and she desired a relationship with him. Jessica thought about those "pockets of grace" Teri spoke of the day the groceries appeared. Nestled among the thick sleeping bags, Jessica felt as if she had fallen literally into one of those pockets of grace. Closing her eyes, she slept.

Forty minutes or so passed. Yet her sleep felt as if it had lasted hours, long enough to give her a second wind and the mental strength to think through what she should do next. Crawling from her little pocket, Jessica looked out both windows. No twisted faces awaited her. She reviewed the situation. Their goods had been pillaged from the back of the truck, but hopefully, the others would see that those were only things, things that could be replaced. She could leave the truck and try walking to the main road, but it was just past midnight and inky black outside. There was also the mud and rain to consider. At least she was dry and fairly protected in the locked cab of the truck. The best she could do was sit and wait. And pray.

"God," she spoke into the stillness, "thank you." Jessica paused and then started to laugh at herself for speaking to someone who was invisible. "I hope you understand this is all new to me." Jessica shifted her position on the cab bench seat. "Obviously you do, since you know everything. I just don't want to ever lose this feeling, this awareness of you."

For quite some time Jessica sat peacefully, taking inventory of her life. Things were still complicated. Very complicated. Every so often a fearful thought flickered across her mind. What if the men came back for the rest of the loot? Would the "banditos" break her windows the next time? How long would it take before Kyle noticed she wasn't behind him? When would he turn around and come back? Would he be able to find her on this desolate dirt road?

Suddenly, headlights shone through the driving rain down the road in front of her. Jessica's first impulse was to jump out of the car and flag down the driver. Then she realized it could be the thieves returning. Would her hiding place keep her safe a second time?

Jessica dropped to the floor and covered herself with sleeping bags. Her heart began to beat frantically. She felt overwhelmed with as much fear as she had experienced the first time, if not more, because now she knew the chances were greater they would come after the sleeping bags. She couldn't pray. She couldn't think. For a moment she felt she couldn't even breathe.

The vehicle stopped. A car door slammed. The noise of the rain on the roof and hood of the truck masked the sound of the voices that had been so boisterous the last time. Jessica pressed her quivering lips together as the handle of the driver's door rattled. It rattled some more, and then Jessica's heart stopped. They had managed to open the door!

Chapter Seventeen

The door of the cab opened slowly. There were no sounds. No movement. No voices. Had they seen her? Jessica felt her whole body shake. She closed her eyes and begged God to save her.

"Jess? Jessica? Are you in here?"

"Kyle?"

"Where are you?"

Jessica forced her paralyzed fists to open and push away the sleeping bags. "Down here. I'm down here." She crawled out of her pocket and up onto the seat where Kyle was leaning over, reaching out a strong hand to help her up.

"Are you okay?"

Jessica let Kyle pull her all the way up. She impulsively threw her arms around his neck and began to sob.

"What happened, Jess?" he spoke softly, wrapping his arms around her and pressing his lips against her ear.

A wave of a new emotion washed over Jessica, and she

pulled away. With both fists clenched, she pounded Kyle's chest. "You left me, that's what happened! Why did you leave me?"

Kyle grabbed both her wrists and held them fast. "I didn't know." His words were firm. "I didn't see you leave the road."

"A truck cut in front of me, and I followed it here." She began to cry again. "I blinked, but you didn't stop."

"I thought you were behind me. I didn't realize I'd lost you. I'm so sorry, Jessica. It must have been terrifying to be stuck here."

"They came and looted the truck," she said, controlling her tears and pulling the rein in on her emotions.

"Who came?" Kyle stroked her hair and wiped her tears with his steady hand.

"Some men. They broke open the back of the truck. I don't know what's left."

Kyle pulled Jessica to his chest and held her close. "Oh, Jess, I'm sorry. No wonder you were hiding. They didn't see you?"

"I don't think so. I thought you were them. Coming back for these sleeping bags." Jessica could hear Kyle's heart beating with a thick, steady rhythm as she surrendered herself to his embrace. They held each other silently for a minute before Kyle pulled away. He had one leg still outside the truck, one leg bent under the steering wheel, and his arms stretched across the seat to hold her.

"I'm going to see what they took. I'll be right back."

"I'm going with you," Jessica said, slipping across the seat and joining Kyle outside in the rain, which had slowed to a drizzle. Kyle put his arm around her shoulders, and they walked through the mushy mud to the back of the truck. The lock on the back had been broken off, and the door was still rolled up. All that was left were the two empty ice chests, three pieces of luggage, and one sleeping bag.

"Wow, they sure cleaned us out," Kyle said. Jessica wondered if he would be upset at the loss. He seemed to take it in stride. "I'm just glad you're okay," he said, wrapping his arms around her once more.

Jessica circled his middle with her arms and leaned her head against his shoulder. She thought of how good Kyle felt and how she fit so perfectly in his embrace. She belonged here. *Don't ever let go.*

"What I think we should do," Kyle said, "is load up what's left in the back of the van and drive back to Mexicali. The rest of the group is at the border control station. We can't pull the truck out of the mud tonight. We'll go to a motel on the American side of the border, and then I'll come back in the morning with a tow truck."

Jessica helped load the luggage into the van. Kyle locked the truck with his second set of keys and did his best to close the broken door on the back so it would at least keep out the rain. Jessica hopped up into the front passenger seat of the van, and Kyle turned the key in the ignition.

Nothing happened. He tried again. All they heard was a faint clicking sound.

"I don't believe this!" Kyle said, banging his fist on the steering wheel. "It sounds like the battery." He popped the hood, fished under the front seat for a flashlight, and then hopped out in the rain to examine the stubborn beast. "Try starting it now," he called to Jessica.

She reached over and turned the key. Nothing.

"Try it now."

She did and again nothing.

Kyle slammed the hood and hustled back into the front seat, shaking the wet from his jacket before hopping in. "I don't know what the problem is."

They were silent for a moment.

"I guess we're stuck," he said. "It'll be daylight in about…," he checked his watch with the flashlight, "four hours. We can walk out to the main road for help then. It would be foolish for us to try it now."

"What about Teri and the rest of the group?" Jessica asked.

"They'll be okay. At least I know where they are. They have shelter, couches, and a candy bar machine. That's more than we have," Kyle said.

Jessica wanted to say, "But I have you, and I feel safe now." Instead she said, "I'm glad you found me."

"I have to tell you," Kyle said, turning so that his back rested against the closed door, and he was facing Jessica, "I was pretty scared there for awhile."

"*You* were scared!" Jessica said, following Kyle's example and leaning against her closed door to face him. "This night ranks among the very worst of my life." Then remembering her conversations with God, she added, "And I guess it also ranks among the very best."

"What do you mean?"

Now Jessica wasn't sure what to say. She thought Kyle would be pleased about this milestone on her spiritual journey, yet she didn't know how to express it. Kyle waited patiently while she searched for the words. Finally she said, "I sort of came to terms with God. I guess you could say that in my spiritual journey I've fallen on my face."

In the darkness, she couldn't see Kyle's face. She sensed a deeper warmth in his voice as he said, "And?"

"And…I've surrendered. It's a big step for me, trusting God like this. He never really seemed to be on my side before."

"But now you're on his side," Kyle suggested.

Jessica nodded. "I don't know how to say it, but I know everything is different."

Kyle reached across the open space between the two seats and grasped Jessica's hand. He squeezed it three times, and in a rather hoarse voice he said, "I am so, so glad. Eternity begins tonight, Jess. You're saved."

She thought those were awfully bold words. Yet his hand felt warm and secure blanketing hers.

"You're cold," Kyle said. "Let me get you a sleeping bag." He crawled to the back of the van and brought back two sleeping bags. Unzipping the first one, Kyle placed it over Jessica and tucked part of the puffy down bag behind her back. He used the second one as a back rest between himself and the cold window on the driver's side. Then, looping his left arm over the top of the steering wheel, he asked, "Do you want to try to sleep?"

Jessica couldn't help but admire Kyle's chivalrous acts. What she really wanted to do was talk. She had let herself become more vulnerable with Kyle than she ever had intended. She didn't know what would happen to them back in the "real world," where she had to carefully guard herself.

However, tonight, for the next four hours, they were alone. Completely alone. If ever she had an opportunity to find out about this man, it was now. She wasn't sure what she would do with the information. She knew she shouldn't process it in terms of Kyle being someone she would become attached to. That would mean she would have to tell him the truth about her life, and she couldn't do that. For now, she could listen. She could hear from Kyle's own lips why he was interested in her and why he had so patiently pursued her.

Before she lost her courage, Jessica said, "What I'd really like to do is listen to you."

"Listen to me?"

"Yes, tell me about you."

"What do you want to know?"

"About your family."

"I have two younger brothers. One is a year younger, the other, three. My parents have been married for thirty-five years and have lived in the same house in Portland for thirty-one of those years. My father was a pilot. What else do you want to know?"

"What do you want to tell me?"

Kyle laughed. "I have a dog," he said. "She's the only other family member. Her name is Amber. She's a golden retriever. Do you like dogs?"

"Sure. I like golden retrievers. They're beautiful." Jessica felt snug under the warm sleeping bag. She was trying to picture what it would be like to go hiking or camping with Kyle and have Amber curl up beside her at the campfire at night.

"What about you?" Kyle asked.

"I don't have a dog," Jessica said.

"I know you don't have a dog. What about your family?"

"Well," Jessica began slowly, "my mom died when I was eight. My dad is a businessman, and I grew up in southern California. There's not much to tell. I always wanted to live in a small town and be a teacher. I guess I'm doing what I've always wanted." She hoped Kyle would be satisfied with her answer and not probe any further. She quickly thought of a question for him. "Did you always want to be a firefighter?"

"Don't all little boys?" Kyle said. "Actually, I came by it in an unusual way. I thought about being a school counselor or football coach because I liked teenagers and I wanted to work with them. But then, about four years ago, I ended up taking care of an elderly woman for awhile, and I decided I wanted to help people medically and then volunteer my time to work with teens. And that's what I'm doing."

Jessica surmised that the elderly woman was Thelma. She

wanted to hear more. "Was the woman ill?" she ventured, wondering if she should come right out and tell him that she knew about Thelma.

"She had cancer."

"Tell me the whole story," Jessica said. "I'd really like to hear it."

Kyle let out a heavy sigh. "Her name was Thelma Atkins. She was the dearest woman you would ever hope to meet. She prayed for me every day. I don't mean a little sentence. She prayed for hours. An amazing woman." For the next ten minutes Kyle proceeded to tell Jessica about Thelma and repeated what Dawn had already told her about Lindsey coming to help out and then dying a few months before Thelma did.

"You and Lindsey were engaged?" Jessica asked, since Kyle hadn't yet used that term.

"Yes. She was only nineteen when we got engaged. I suppose we thought we knew what we were doing. Our engagement didn't even last two months before she died."

"What did she die of?" Jessica asked.

Kyle didn't answer. Jessica remembered that Dawn said it was pneumonia. In the darkness, Jessica couldn't tell if Kyle had floated off in his memory or if he had clammed up. His words had seemed so intimate and sincere up to this point. Jessica wasn't sure if she had overstepped her boundaries. It didn't bother her to hear about Lindsey. She felt the same sympathetic camaraderie as she had in the graveyard when thinking of her mother's death.

"I'm sorry if I'm being too nosy," Jessica said.

"No, that's all right." Kyle paused and then said, "Lindsey died of AIDS."

Jessica never expected to hear that.

"No one knows," Kyle added quickly. "I'm not sure why I

felt I could tell you. Besides Dr. Laughlin, who maintains professional confidentiality, no one else in Glenbrooke knows. Thelma never knew. It would have broken her heart."

Jessica couldn't think of what to say. "I'm sorry," were the only words that came from her mouth. But her mind was flooded with a thousand questions. Jessica had felt one thing thinking of a beautiful young woman dying of pneumonia, but she experienced a completely different reaction hearing she had died of AIDS.

"Are you okay?" Jessica asked tentatively, feeling that the question could be taken in a non-probing way, or could lead Kyle to open up about his own state of health.

"If you mean about her death, I think so. It's taken me a long time to get over her, but I think I finally am." Kyle drew in a deep breath. "If you mean do I have AIDS, no. I don't. Lindsey and I were never intimate. She got it from a football player in high school. She was fifteen; he was a senior. He chased her for a month until she finally went out with him. They went out twice. He got what he wanted on their second date and then dropped her to go out with the head cheerleader. It's a pretty typical high school scenario. Lindsey didn't know what was going on. She was so innocent. She was chaste after that. But all it takes is once."

Jessica could tell Kyle was struggling from the way his voice wavered. She reached over and held his hand lightly as he finished his story.

"I met her when she came to Glenbrooke to take care of her grandmother. We dated for four months, and then I asked her to marry me. The day after we bought her engagement ring, Lindsey received a phone call from this guy. He was in the hospital in Spokane, and he told her he had AIDS and was trying to contact every girl he had slept with. I imagine the list was rather long. He told her he was sorry. He died four months after she did."

"How awful," Jessica said, holding Kyle's hand a little tighter.

"I can't believe I'm telling you this," Kyle said. "I've never told anyone. No one. Not even my mother."

"I'm glad you're telling me," Jessica said softly. She remembered what Kyle had said to her that afternoon when she told him to leave her alone. "I think I understand now why you said secrets get heavier the longer you carry them. I'm glad you're not carrying this all alone anymore."

"This isn't public information, though," Kyle said, leaning forward. "I need you to keep this confidential, Jessica. It would shock too many people if they knew the truth."

"And it probably wouldn't do too much for your reputation either, would it?"

Kyle pulled his hand away.

"I'm sorry," Jessica said quickly. "That didn't come out the way I meant it. You have a lot of friends in Glenbrooke, and people look up to you. A stigma comes with AIDS. People might look at you differently if they knew."

"Do you?"

"No." She reached for his hand again. "Kyle, I know this whole thing had to be unbelievably difficult for you, and I know all about carrying heavy secrets. Knowing this doesn't change my opinion of you. Honest. It makes me admire you even more for all you've gone through." She paused. "May I ask you something?"

"Okay."

"What if you knew you could save someone's life. You would do it, wouldn't you?"

"Of course."

"I know you would. I mean, you came to my rescue, and you took care of Mrs. Atkins. Kyle, what if you could save someone's life, like Dawn Laughlin's?"

"What are you getting at, Jessica?" She heard an edge of irritation in his voice.

"Dozens of young girls like Lindsey are fifteen right now. You could have such an influence on their lives that they would never have to worry about receiving a phone call when they're nineteen." Jessica wasn't sure if she had overstepped her boundaries. Kyle had turned quiet, and his hand didn't move. Jessica gave it a little squeeze and said, "I could be completely out of line here, but Kyle, if you came to my health ed class and told your story, I think it would have a profound effect on the students. All I can give them are statistics. You can give them reality."

Kyle pulled his hand away and ran his fingers through his hair. Jessica sat back, leaning against the door. *Why did you drop such a bomb on him? Now you've pushed him away. What a stupid thing to do, Jessica!*

"I'll think about it," he said quietly. "You just don't know how hard that would be."

Gathering her courage, Jessica let her convictions all hang out. "Kyle, I think it would be harder if you found out three or four years from now that one of the guys or girls on this trip had AIDS when you had had it in your power to do something to try to prevent it."

In the darkness Jessica sat still, listening to the chorus of vehement accusations raging in her head. Why did she have to be so outspoken all of a sudden? After weeks of controlling her tongue and her true personality, why did she have to hit Kyle with both barrels? And what right did she have to suggest someone expose his secret when she was still holding on to hers? She wouldn't blame the guy if he pushed her out in the rain and told her to walk home.

"You're right," he said in a quavering voice. "I long ago passed the point in which I'm protecting Thelma or trying to honor Lindsey's memory. I've been trying to protect myself."

Chapter Eighteen

To be honest takes a lot of nerve. But to be direct and blunt borders on being nervy. Jessica couldn't believe she had spoken to Kyle so mercilessly. She wished she would have just listened. Isn't that what a good friend does? Be sympathetic, but don't challenge. Don't rock the boat. Listen and nod your understanding.

"Kyle," she spoke in a voice barely above a whisper, "I'm sorry." Within her was an overpowering urge to fly into his arms, to hold him close and to comfort him. She wasn't sure what kept her on her side of the van. She was even less sure why she had challenged him to take his painful secret and wave it like a banner in front of the gentle people of Glenbrooke.

Then she thought again of Dawn, a sincerely searching young woman. One hour with the wrong guy could destroy her whole life. "I come on a little too strong sometimes. I'm sorry," was all Jessica said.

She heard a sniff and then a cough as Kyle cleared his throat. "You don't know what this means to me, Jess. The day I met you, the day of your accident, I was coming back from a sort of personal retreat. I went camping for three days by myself and asked the Lord for two things. First, that I would be able to get on with my life. For the past four years I've mourned the loss, and I haven't been able to move on to any other relationships. Then I asked God to take all this pain and turn it into something good. I never thought of talking with teens about it. I was always so concerned about protecting Lindsey and Thelma. But you're right. Part of me was protecting myself, too. I need to think about others, about how I can turn this into a way to help them."

"Still," Jessica said, feeling as if he hadn't heard her apology, "you could have come to that conclusion without me pouncing on you so unsympathetically. I tend to be pretty goal-oriented once I get an idea in my head."

"Don't you see," Kyle said, the rich, warm tones returning to his voice, "God used you to help me see it. I needed to hear your ideas. As for the sympathy, that's all I've gotten from anyone in Glenbrooke for the past four years. Everyone feels sorry for me. They all say they admire me. Fine. Now let me move on!"

Just then a set of headlights came toward them. Kyle squinted and tried to see what kind of vehicle it was.

"What if it's the robbers?" Jessica asked. She didn't feel afraid.

"It looks like a sedan, not a truck. Could be that help has arrived." Kyle stepped out of the truck and waved his arms over his head at the oncoming car. It had stopped raining. In the light provided by the other car, Jessica could see just how thick the mud was on the side of the road and how slushy the gravel had become. The car stopped, and Kyle spoke to the driver, pointing at both vehicles and then pointing again to the van. A few minutes later he jogged back to the van as the car drove away.

"Well?" Jessica asked.

"He's going home and said he would call a tow truck in the morning."

"A village is at the end of this road?" Jessica asked.

"There must be. Even though it's gravel, this looks like a fairly well traveled road. He invited us to stay at his house, but I told him we would rather stay here. I hope you don't mind."

Jessica thought of the tiny adobe houses in Nueva and the way the chickens and pigs ran freely across the dirt floors. "Good choice," she said. "I think the van is just fine."

"Yeah, well I wish the van was just fine enough to drive us back to the border. You know, it really gets to me when we end up having to use undependable vehicles for this trip. Two years ago we rented a van that overheated on the way down and nearly blew up."

"Why don't you rent different vans? Something newer, maybe."

"Money," Kyle said flatly. "If we had the money I'd do a lot of things differently."

"Like what?"

"Like the vans. I'd pay the extra and go with a rental company that only had late model vehicles. And if I had the money, I'd make sure the next time we start a building project we can do it all in one trip and not make the people wait a year before we finish what we've begun. I've thought through all the things I would do—if I had more money. I'm a dreamer," he said with a laugh.

"What's your dream?" Jessica asked.

"Do you really want to know?"

"Yes, I do."

"My dream is to have a million dollars. Not even a million.

I could do it all with about $500,000."

"Do what?" Jessica asked again.

She could hear the excitement in his voice. "First, I'd build an orphanage down here. Probably in Nueva. And I'd hire qualified staff to take care of the kids. Then, I'd set up a scholarship fund for teenagers. I know a lot of bright students in Glenbrooke who should be going to college, but they won't. Their parents work at the mill or in the little shops around town, and the money isn't there to send them to college."

"That sounds good," Jessica agreed.

"And if there's any money left over, I have two good friends who are missionaries in Kenya. They live on so little. I'd like to underwrite their expenses so the mission school doesn't shut down every few months because they've run out of funds."

Jessica thought that Kyle had to be the most noble man she had ever met. To wish for half a million dollars to give it away was incredible to her.

"You know what I just realized?" Kyle said, reaching over and taking Jessica by the hand. "For the past hour or so, all we've done is talk about me. What about you? Tell me about Jessica."

"What do you want to know?" She wondered if the sudden sense of guardedness showed up in her voice.

"Well, let's start with your wishes. What would you do if you had a million dollars?"

"A million dollars?" Jessica said, tension creeping up her spine. "Um, I don't know. Buy a house, I suppose."

"What kind of house?"

"Just a cozy little house. One with a purple hydrangea bush in the front."

Kyle laughed. "I tell you what. If God ever blesses me with half a million dollars, I'll buy you a cozy little house with two purple hydrangea bushes!"

Jessica knew he was teasing, yet she felt uncomfortable even thinking about being on the receiving end of someone's charity. Jessica laughed and hoped Kyle didn't noticed how forced and nervous it sounded. "And if I get a million dollars, I promise I'll buy you an orphanage, a scholarship fund, and what was the other one?"

"Kenya," Kyle said.

"Oh, yes, I'll buy you Kenya."

They laughed. When the air between them turned hushed once more, Kyle leaned over and took both of Jessica's hands in his.

"Jess," he said firmly. She could see the serious expression on his face in the dim green light from the digital clock on the dashboard. "I know a lot has gone on for you on this trip and even before this. I'd like to think that you and I are both at a place where we can start spending time together. Would you feel comfortable with that? I'd really like to get to know you."

"Well, I'm not really, I mean…it's not a good…" Jessica found it impossible to say no to this man as he held her hand.

"Don't try to answer me now. I don't know what things you're working through, but I'll wait for you." Kyle gave her hands three squeezes and then let go.

"I'll come to your health ed class next week or whenever it works out for you. And I want you to know that I can be a pretty good listener, too. You've seen how deeply my secret has affected me. It's amazing how different everything seems now that I've told you. I don't know what you're carrying around, Jessica. If ever you want someone to share the load, I want to be there for you."

Kyle had been so honest with her, she felt she had to tell him her secret. She had to say *something*.

"It's my dad," she spouted. "I have some problems with my dad, and I need to stay away from him."

"Can I ask what you've done to work things out? Do you need to call in a professional of some sort?" Kyle ventured.

Jessica shook her head. "No, my dad is surrounded by professionals. He doesn't need another one. And he doesn't need me. The easiest way to explain it is to say that he and I differ on how I should live my life. I have to keep my identity and my whereabouts a secret. I know that may sound like a low-budget spy movie or something, but it's the only way I can live the kind of life I want. That's why I changed my name to Fenton." She felt relieved telling Kyle a few of her secrets. But she hoped he wouldn't probe any deeper.

"By the way," Jessica asked, "how did you find out my real last name was Morgan?"

"Ida. When I picked up the key to your house, she said Hugh had rented it to Jessica Morgan."

Jessica felt relieved that innocent Ida had been the source of the information and not Charlotte, or Jessica's wallet, or the luggage tag.

"So you still haven't answered my question," Kyle said.

"What's that?"

"Will you go out with me? Maybe to dinner or a movie or something when we get back?"

Jessica waged war with her common sense and her softening emotions. She heard herself say, "Yes, I'd love to go out with you."

A tow truck of sorts arrived shortly after seven o'clock and pulled the truck from the mud. Kyle and several Mexican men who stopped by the van on their way to work in the fields labored over the engine and found a wire had jiggled loose. By 7:30, with the sun breaking through the clouds and going about its task of drying up the earth, Kyle and Jessica were back on the main road, headed for Mexicali.

This time Jessica had no difficulty following the van all the way to the border, where a line of cars had already formed. They had to sit and wait along with the rest of the motorists. Insistent street vendors walked between the cars showing their wares. Everything from that day's newspaper to pottery piggy banks paraded past Jessica's closed truck window. Each time a vendor motioned to her, she would smile and shake her head. Jessica noticed that Kyle kept handing money out his window to salespeople, especially the children.

Several raggedly dressed boys shimmied up on Kyle's front bumper and with dirty, wet rags attempted to wash his window. Kyle paid them and soon vendors seemed to appear at the van from out of nowhere. Jessica watched as Kyle dealt with each of them generously. Once again she found herself impressed with this man. She felt thrilled at the thought of spending time with Kyle when they got back to Glenbrooke, yet at the same time she felt guilty about starting something she knew she couldn't finish.

The rest of the group had endured the night in their muddy clothes at the border station and were incredulous when they learned their suitcases had been stolen and they couldn't change.

"Whose suitcases were left?" Bill asked. "Not that it matters. I kind of like the idea of boarding a plane in San Diego looking and smelling like a homeless person. If I carry a cup around, I might even make some money at the airport."

One of the bags was Teri's, one was Jessica's, and the third belonged to Brenda, who Jessica noticed had become rather chummy with Bill. Teri's advice must have paid off. Jessica couldn't help but wonder if Teri would have some advice for her once she found out that Jessica had agreed to go out with Kyle.

"So much for any of the guys borrowing clean clothes," Bill moaned. He looked pretty grubby, but that didn't stop Brenda from sitting next to him in the van on the way to San Diego. Jessica drove the truck again, only this time Teri joined her.

"It sounds as if you had quite a night out on the lonesome prairie," Teri said once they were on their way to San Diego.

Jessica put together some sketchy phrases to explain she had spent the time soul searching and that she had made a commitment to Christ. Teri screamed, hugged Jessica, and bounced up and down in her seat. Tears raced down her cheeks while she laughed.

Jessica began to realize this might be a bigger, more important decision than she had initially thought. She decided to hold off telling Teri about going out with Kyle.

Teri found out soon enough, though. When they were back at school on Tuesday, trying to shake their culture shock and get back in the swing of things, Kyle stopped by Jessica's room after school when Teri was there. He asked Jessica out to dinner on Friday night and if Wednesday afternoon would be a good time for him to come to her health ed class. When Jessica agreed to both, Teri's eyes grew wide. Kyle offered to take Jessica home. She could tell that Teri was dying to know what was going on. Kyle dropped Jessica in front of her house without coming in, since he had to get back to the station. And, as Jessica almost could have guessed, Teri appeared on her doorstep a slim five minutes later.

"I noticed there weren't any cars out front," Teri said with a twinkle in her eye. "So I thought I'd stop by and see if there might possibly be anything you would like to chat about."

"Would you like a cup of tea?" Jessica asked, grinning widely.

"Don't mind if I do." Teri hobbled into the house on her sprained ankle.

"Feel free to put up your foot," Jessica said. "I'll be right back with some tea."

Teri was on her way to the couch when the phone, which was sitting on the coffee table, rang. "Do you want me to get it?" Teri asked.

"Sure," Jessica called back from the kitchen. Teri didn't call Jessica to the phone, so she waited for the water in the tea kettle to boil, poured it over the Good Earth tea bag, and carried the two mugs into the living room on a tray.

"Who was on the phone?"

"Wrong number," Teri said. "Somebody named Greg Fletcher trying to contact a Jessica Morgan."

Jessica abruptly lowered the tray to the coffee table, rattling both the cups in the process.

"Whoa!" Teri said, reaching for one of the mugs before it spilled. "Got it." She drew the hot mug to her lips for a sip and then looked at Jessica, who was still standing. "Jess, are you okay?"

Chapter Nineteen

*J*essica sat down and tried to calmly sip her tea. She changed the subject from the phone call to Kyle. "He said he wants to take me to a Chinese restaurant. Do you want to come with us? I'm sure it would be fine with Kyle."

Teri shook her head, laughing at Jessica's suggestion. "I think he would rather it be just the two of you. Don't downplay this, Jess. You have to realize you're the first woman in four years he has asked out. That's no small thing, especially with a man like Kyle, who in my opinion, is the catch of the century."

"Then why didn't you ever go out with him?" Jessica asked.

"No chemistry," Teri said, holding up her left hand and flicking her fingers several times in the air. "No sparks. We settled into the brother-sister role from the beginning and neither of us tried to move it to anything else."

"Then who does make sparks for you?" Jessica asked, eager to get the focus off herself.

"He's not from around here. His name is Mark. Mark Hunter."

"And where is this Mark Hunter?"

"Hawaii," Teri said with a playful smile curling up the corners of her mouth. "One of my sisters moved there, and I went to visit her this summer. They set me up with Mark the first night, we were together as much as possible for the next week and a half, and then I came home."

"You two really hit it off?"

Teri nodded and smiled. "Chemistry," she said. "Sparks-a-plenty."

"So why haven't you pursued anything?"

"Mark is a marine biologist. He's working on a grant for a year studying whales and the way they communicate with each other. It's really pretty fascinating. I happened to be there the week before his program started, so he had some time for me. Now he's buried in his research until next July." Teri sipped the last of her tea and added, "I do have three Hallmark cards and two phone calls to brag about. But I've set the relationship aside until next summer."

"Are you planning to go back to Hawaii in July, then?" Jessica asked.

"I might go as soon as school is out. I've been saving every penny. We'll see what God has in mind. Right now he seems awfully silent when I talk to him about Mark."

"I hope things work out for you," Jessica said.

"I do, too." Teri placed her mug on the tray and rose to leave. "Thanks for the tea and sympathy," she said, shooting her bright smile at Jessica and hobbling toward the door. "This stupid ankle. What a nuisance! I twisted it when I was in high school at cheerleader tryouts, and since then I've sprained it probably five times. You would think I'd be used to it by now. I do own a rather interesting assortment of ankle braces and bandages. Well, I'll see you tomorrow. Bye."

Teri left, and Jessica returned to the kitchen where she placed the mugs in the sink and looked at her hands. They were quivering.

Should I call Greg? What would I say? How did he find me? What if something is wrong with my father?

Jessica went to the secretary and pulled out her address book. She thumbed through the pages until she found the number and dialed it quickly.

"Good afternoon. Fletcher, Holcomb, and Meiers."

Jessica couldn't speak.

"Hello?"

"Yes," she said, trying to steady her voice, "Greg Fletcher, please."

"May I tell Mr. Fletcher who's calling?"

Without thinking, Jessica hung up. *This is ridiculous! What am I doing? I can't contact Greg. Not yet.*

For the rest of the week, Jessica wondered why Greg Fletcher had called. Yet she refused to phone him back.

On Wednesday, Kyle came to her health ed class as promised. She knew his talk would be important to himself and to the teens. What she didn't realize was how powerful his words would be. As Kyle told the class about Lindsey and how she contracted AIDS—just one time, from one guy—girls were sniffling and guys were leaning back in their chairs with their arms across their chests as they studied Kyle with somber expressions. The portion of Kyle's presentation that surprised her most was when he told the class he was a virgin. She hadn't expected a twenty-six-year-old man like Kyle to have made it this far as a virgin and then to talk about it openly. Jessica thought no man on earth could be a more powerful example of virtue and chastity. Not for these students.

She was even more convinced of how right she had been

to invite Kyle to speak when she overhead two of her students in the back of the class. One of the girls was tearfully telling her friend, "If I thought a guy like Kyle might be waiting for me—intact—when I finished school, I never would have done it with Andy."

"That's behind you," the other girl said. "You can still hold out for a hero. Starting today. You can be pure from here on out. It's not too late."

Jessica wondered if she should try to enter into their conversation, but decided they were doing just fine.

When Kyle was about to leave her room, he gave Jessica a look she had never seen before on his face, as if he were experiencing pain and joy at the same time. Bittersweet lines of victory and hope were drawn across his forehead. Jessica's anticipation for Friday, when they went out to dinner and could talk, grew more intense.

She found herself considering telling Kyle about the phone call from Greg Fletcher. But how could she mention that her dad's lawyer called and she had struggled with calling him back unless she unloaded her whole history on Kyle? And she couldn't do that. She hated the position she was in. She hadn't counted on someone like Kyle coming into her life when she made her decision to tuck her past away forever.

Wednesday night Kyle called Jessica from the station. "My schedule has changed. I have tomorrow off, and I was wondering if you would be up for getting together tomorrow night."

Jessica wondered if Kyle was beginning to feel the way she did—that it was too long to wait until Friday to see each other. She accepted, and he said he would pick her up after school. The Chinese restaurant he wanted to take her to was an hour away.

"You'll love this place," he said. "They have the best kung pao chicken in Oregon. It's well worth the drive."

Jessica dressed with extra care on Thursday morning and walked to school under the cloudy skies with a song in her heart. She passed the hydrangea bush where her little squirrels lived and noticed how all the lavender snowballs had transformed into dried up brown wads. How short had been their bright blooming season. A familiar fear crept in and began to torture Jessica, the fear that what she had allowed to begin with Kyle would only be a bright burst and then be gone.

In the past few days she had noticed a definite peace overriding her other emotions, an indication, she knew, of her changed view of God. However, her everyday life was still a tangled mess. She couldn't impose any of that on Kyle.

Jessica walked into her classroom a few minutes before eight o'clock. Charlotte Mendelson sat on the corner of her desk. "You have a problem, Ms. Morgan-Fenton," Charlotte began. "Did you have a guest speaker in your health ed class yesterday?"

"Yes." Jessica set down her tote bag and approached Charlotte with confidence. "It was the best thing I've done all year."

"You didn't clear it with me, you didn't clear the topic with the school board, and you didn't send home the required letter to the parents ahead of time." Charlotte rose, threw back her shoulders, and towered over Jessica. "Disciplinary action will be discussed at the next school board meeting. You'll receive a notice." Clicking her tall, narrow heels and striding to the door, Charlotte tossed over her shoulder, "I am going to see to it that you are ousted from this school before the month is over."

Before Jessica could gather her wits about her, students began to file into the classroom. *Let it go, Jess,* she coached herself. *Don't let that woman get to you. The school board will understand when they hear how much good Kyle's talk did. Charlotte doesn't have anything on you.*

Dawn came up to Jessica's desk and said, "Could I talk to you a minute in private?"

"Sure."

They hovered in a corner at the back of the room. Dawn spoke in hushed tones, flipping her long hair first to one side of her head and then to the other. "I just wanted to tell you thanks for having Kyle talk to us yesterday. He really made me think. I didn't know about Lindsey. Nobody did, I guess. After everything I learned in Mexico last weekend and the friends I made, I feel as if things are turning around in my life. And then Kyle's talk yesterday—I have a different perspective on life. I know I probably sounded pretty weird when I came to your house a few weeks ago. Things are a lot clearer for me now, and you had a big part in that. I just want to say thanks."

Jessica repeated Dawn's words to Kyle that night as they drove to dinner. She also told him about Charlotte. Kyle's advice was not to worry about Charlotte.

"Oh, I know," Jessica agreed. "I won't let her get under my skin. But I thought you should know what she said in case the school board calls you in on this."

A smile spread across Kyle's broad jaw, and he shot a glance at Jessica. "It won't be a problem," he said confidently. Jessica wished she could have the same optimism.

Once they were seated in a red vinyl booth at the rather small Chinese restaurant, Jessica opened her tall menu and scanned the items listed. It was an extensive list, especially for such a remote restaurant. "How did you ever find this place?" she asked Kyle.

"A couple of us guys stumbled on it when we came back

from a hunting trip last fall. What do you think? Pretty authentic, isn't it?"

Jessica wasn't sure what he meant by authentic. She ordered the sweet and sour pork and a dish of steamed dumplings, which they shared. The food was good. Yet to Jessica the food mattered little. Being with Kyle was what was good. She listened to him talk about deer season in Oregon and camping in the winter in Idaho on the ice.

"Oh, I almost forgot to tell you the good news," he said. "The border patrol in Calexico called this morning. They found the guys who took all our stuff. They were trying to sell a major portion of it to one person, and the guy turned them in."

"That's amazing," Jessica said. "Were most of the items still there?"

"I don't know. We'll find out. They boxed it all up and put it on a bus. It'll be here Monday."

"That's great, Kyle! I hope you get all your camping gear back."

"Me, too. I don't exactly have the money to go out and replace all of it. Do you want to try some of this?" He pointed his wooden chopsticks at a still steaming mound of chicken and fried rice.

"Sure."

Kyle scooped up a lump of rice on his chopsticks and precariously held it in midair between them. Jessica leaned over and tried to gracefully make contact with the rice. Most of it went in her mouth as she suppressed a laugh. Kyle smiled and reached across with his other hand, gently wiping a few stray grains from her top lip.

His touch on her lip had a powerful effect on her. His finger, her lip. It had been their first meeting point. Jessica caught her breath and looked away.

She poked around at her pork, trying to squelch the desire to speak openly with Kyle, to release the burden on her heart and be freed from it the way Kyle appeared to be free from the secret of Lindsey's death.

"Jess, I want to ask you something."

Jessica looked up at him and tried to smooth all the worry lines off her forehead.

"Can you tell me why you left California? What is it you're running from?"

"Like I told you in Mexico. My dad."

Kyle waited for her to continue, but she didn't. "Can the relationship be healed?"

"I don't think so. Not unless I go back. And I won't."

They ate silently. A huge knot formed in Jessica's stomach. She found it hard to eat and put down her chopsticks. Cupping both hands around the small teacup, Jessica sipped her tea. The waiter brought the check and a plate with two fortune cookies.

Jessica chose one, hoping the silly proverb inside would allow them a new topic of conversation. She cracked it open, pulled out the white slip of paper, and read it to herself.

"What does it say?" Kyle asked.

"It says, 'Do not seek fame. It will find you.' Now those are profound words!"

Kyle opened his fortune cookie and read aloud, "In matters of love, remain firm."

"Ooh," Jessica teased. "Mr. Tough Guy, huh?"

"You heard it here first," Kyle said. He reached for his wallet, and Jessica watched him inconspicuously tuck the slip of paper into his wallet as he took out his Visa and flipped it down on the check. She thought it was sweet and sentimental of him to save the fortune and decided to do the same with hers.

"Would you like to go to the football game with me tomorrow night?" Kyle asked once they were back in the truck and on their way home. "You haven't seen our guys defend their title yet, have you?"

"Sure, I'd love to." Jessica slid across the bench seat in the front of the truck and sat closer to Kyle.

Kyle responded the way she had hoped he would. He slid his arm across the back of the seat and enveloped her shoulder with his large hand. Jessica snuggled a little closer and comfortably rested her head against his shoulder. It was wonderfully relaxing. Neither of them spoke.

The road stretched on and on in front of them, and they sat close as each listened to the steady breathing of the other. With all her heart, Jessica wished this evening could be frozen in time. How she had longed for a man like this and a night like this to be close to him. They didn't have to discuss anything. Not her past, not the future. They had now, and that was all that mattered.

Chapter Twenty

*Y*ou know," Kyle said when they were a few miles outside Glenbrooke, "I never really thanked you for challenging me to be open about Lindsey's death. When you told me about Dawn tonight, I could see that some good has already come from it, and I believe a lot more will."

"I do too," Jessica agreed.

"For one thing," Kyle said softly, "I feel ready and open to pursue a relationship with you. It was a long four years. I can't help but believe God sent you to me."

Jessica felt warmed inside. She had never been anyone's answer to prayer before. Kyle's words comforted and flattered her at the same time. Both were wonderful sensations to lull in while locked into this freeze-frame moment.

"What I'd really like," Kyle said, squeezing Jessica's shoulder, "is to know what you're feeling."

"I love being with you, Kyle. I love listening to you and being close to you like this. And I think in a way God sent you

225

to me. My whole life has changed."

"And for the future?" he asked.

"I don't know," Jessica said, feeling her muscles tighten.

"Jess," Kyle said, his deep voice rumbling in his chest and echoing in her ear, "I don't think you will know until you settle whatever issues you have with your dad."

"It's not that easy," Jessica said, sitting up and putting a few inches of distance between them. "You don't understand what's at stake here."

"I'd like to know, if you would let me," Kyle said.

Jessica shook her head. "I can't. Please try to understand. It's not that I don't wish things were different and that I was free to fall in—" she caught herself. "To be with you."

"You don't have to rephrase it, Jess. I think we both know that we're in love with each other. Why won't you open yourself up with me?"

"Because if I do, then everything will change."

"No it won't. I promise."

"You can't promise," Jessica said, her emotions rising. "You don't even know what you're promising! Can't we just have today and maybe tomorrow and not worry about what comes next?"

"I don't think so," Kyle said. He turned down Jessica's street and brought the truck to an abrupt halt in front of her house. "That's not good enough for me."

"Well then, forget it!" Jessica said, sliding across the seat and opening her own door. "You have no idea what you're asking of me."

She blasted out of the door and slammed it hard. With giant steps, she marched up her front walkway. Surely Kyle would jump out of the truck and come after her. They could work out some kind of middle ground.

But Kyle didn't follow her. As she turned the key in her

door, she heard his tires peel away from the curb and the truck roar down the street. Jessica lurched inside her house and slammed the door. She ripped her purse off her shoulder and threw it on the floor.

"Jessica, you're an idiot!" she yelled. "What are you doing?" She bulldozed her way into the kitchen and poured herself a glass of water. Chugging down the water, she tried to calm herself. *Why did I do that? I'm behaving like a two-year-old. Where is this coming from?*

She had no answers for herself. She only had a wadded up ball of anxiety and energy. She wished she had an exercise bike. She would pedal the entire night if that's what it took to work off this steam. Jessica opted for the stairs instead and began hustling up and down the fourteen steps. Three times, four times. Her breathing and heart rate began to pulsate in time with her emotions. Six times up, six times down. Seven. Eight. At nine ascents and descents, Jessica stopped on the top stair, her heart pounding and her leg aching.

Kyle or no Kyle, she would survive. She never should have let things go as far as they had. She never should have gone to Mexico. But then, she wouldn't have turned her life over to the Lord.

"God?" Jessica panted. "I am doing the right thing, aren't I? You understand, don't you?"

The only thought that came to Jessica was to *surrender.* She didn't like it. She decided to ignore it and take a hot bath and go to bed. She would feel better after a good night's sleep.

Jessica didn't feel better the next morning, because she couldn't sleep. Greg Fletcher had already somehow managed to find her phone number. How long would he be thrown off her trail? And did she really want to live without Kyle? Yet how could she have a relationship with him when he was requiring her to do what she couldn't. She felt cornered.

She struggled to get dressed and mentally prepared for the day. Yesterday she had told her classes they would have a test today, but she hadn't prepared one. Probably none of the students would mind, but she didn't like getting off schedule like this. Especially today, when her nerves were shot.

Jessica hurried out the front door and locked it behind her. When she turned around, she saw Kyle's truck parked at the curb. Kyle was leaning against his vehicle, his arms folded across his chest.

I'm not ready for this. I can't talk to him. Not yet. Not now.

Jessica kept her head down and cut across her front yard, walking briskly down the street toward school. She could hear Kyle coming after her. He fell into step with her and walked silently beside her for half a block before speaking.

"It's no good running, Jess. Let's face this together."

Jessica didn't answer. A thousand possible lines crossed her mind. None of them made it to her lips.

"I have a plane reservation for you," Kyle said. "Portland to Los Angeles. You fly out this afternoon and return Sunday night. I've rented a car for you. Go talk to your dad, Jessica. Straighten this thing out and then come home to me."

Jessica stopped walking and faced Kyle, her face flaming red. "Forget it!" she spouted.

Over their heads a pair of squirrels chittered and scurried across the telephone line, one of them in hot pursuit of the other. It flickered through Jessica's thoughts that being pursued by a relentless tracker wasn't so romantic after all.

"No, you think about it," Kyle said, raising his voice. "I'll pick you up at noon. You'll have to get out of your last few classes, and you'll only have a few minutes to pack. If I didn't care, I wouldn't do this."

Jessica narrowed her eyes and tried to bore her anger into Kyle's steady gaze. He didn't flinch. Like a rock, Kyle stood before her, jaw set, eyes clear, and his expression full of compassion.

"'In matters of love, remain firm,'" Kyle said, quoting his fortune cookie. A smile inched onto his face.

Jessica felt her anger begin to drain from her and a weariness rush in to take its place. She had felt this inner exhaustion for a long time but had refused to acknowledge it. The resources simply weren't available to carry on anymore. "Okay," she whispered, looking down. "Okay."

Kyle cupped her chin in his hand and lifted her face up toward him. He didn't say anything but tenderly rubbed his thumb across the half-moon on her upper lip. This scar that had first brought them together seemed to have as powerful a draw for Kyle as it did for her. Under his touch, she laid down her defenses. All she could think of was the word *surrender.* She still didn't like it.

"I'll be ready at noon," Jessica said, looking up and allowing herself to plunge into Kyle's limpid green gaze.

He drew her close and pressed his cheek against her forehead. She thought he would kiss her, but he didn't. He held her and whispered, "Thank you." The faint scent of cinnamon floated past her nose.

Kyle pulled away and said, "I have to get to the station for a staff meeting. I'll be at the school at noon. Sharp."

"Okay," Jessica said, watching him turn and sprint back to his truck. The interminable little squirrels frolicked down the thick wooden telephone pole and skittered past Jessica, then up a shady elm tree.

She arrived at school a few minutes late and was dismayed to find Charlotte waiting for her again in her classroom, perched once again on Jessica's desk. A few students were already in the classroom. Jessica didn't want them to hear whatever it was their principal had to say.

"You're late," Charlotte said.

Jessica sat in her chair, unlocking her desk and dropping her purse into the bottom drawer without acknowledging Charlotte.

"I had a nice chat with your Aunt Bonnie yesterday," Charlotte said.

Jessica didn't look up. When she had listed Bonnie and John as her nearest relatives, she had gambled that they would never be contacted. Obviously, Charlotte had taken upon herself the role of junior detective.

"She says the whole family has been frantic since you disappeared almost two months ago. None of them seemed to know you were here in Oregon."

Jessica curled her toes inside her shoes and clenched her jaw, waiting for the next bit of information Charlotte had uncovered.

"Bonnie gave me a most interesting phone number." Charlotte read each number slowly and deliberately. "Does that number ring any bells with you, Ms. Morgan?"

It was her father's phone number. His private line.

"I tried him this morning, but Sharon—you know, his secretary, Sharon—well, Sharon said he's just returning from a business trip and will be home later this afternoon." Charlotte leaned over and pointed her finger at Jessica. "Either you tell me what is going on right this instant or I'll fire you!"

"You can't fire me," Jessica said calmly. "That would have to be a board decision."

"Well, after I talk with your father I'm sure I'll have enough information to present to the board at the Monday night meeting." Charlotte was speaking loud enough for the students to hear her. "You did notice your name on the agenda, didn't you?"

"Excuse me," Jessica said, reaching for her purse and rising from her seat. "I don't seem to be feeling very well. It looks as if I'll need to use one of my sick days today."

Jessica walked past Charlotte and out the door. She didn't stop walking until she arrived home. Then she called Kyle at the fire station and told him what had happened.

"You did the right thing," he said. "She was probably trying to force you to quit, the way she tricked Mrs. Blair into quitting. If you *had* quit, getting your job back would be a mess. You're entitled to sick leave. It was a good move, Jess. Do you want to leave now for the airport? I'm pretty sure we can switch you to an earlier flight."

"Okay," Jessica said. "Let me throw some clothes in a suitcase."

"I'll be right over," Kyle said.

"Kyle?"

He had already hung up. Everything was coming at her so fast. She wanted to tell him thanks for setting up this encounter, even though she dreaded it. The meeting with her father was now imperative and inevitable.

Jessica threw some clothes in her garment bag and grabbed her cosmetics from the bathroom. The phone rang as she was zipping up the bag.

"Jess? It's Teri. What's going on? Dawn said Charlotte fired you, and you walked out on the spot."

"No, I'm actually taking a sick day," Jessica said, balancing the portable phone on her shoulder and making a second trip to the closet for another pair of shoes. "I'm going to California. I'll be back Sunday night."

"You're *what?*"

"I don't have time to explain now," Jessica said, hearing Kyle's truck. "I'll talk to you on Monday." She hung up, hoping Teri would accept her hurried explanation.

The phone immediately rang again.

"What do you think you're trying to pull, walking out of your class like that?" Charlotte demanded.

"I came home sick," Jessica said. It wasn't far from the truth. At this moment she was perspiring and felt as if she might throw up. "Teachers are allowed to be sick. It says so in my contract. Please excuse me. I need to hang up now."

Charlotte's voice was raised in anger as Jessica pressed the off button and lugged her garment bag down the stairs. She opened the door just as Kyle knocked. "I'm all ready," she said.

Kyle took her bag from her. "Are you okay? You look a little pale."

"It's been a rather full morning," she said, reaching for her purse and locking the door. She couldn't help but feel like a felon, leaving school in the middle of the morning and hurrying out of town. "Plus I didn't sleep much last night."

Jessica hopped into the truck, and Kyle started down the road toward the highway. She wiped the perspiration from her forehead and rolled down her window. A light rain fell in the window at an angle. She didn't mind. It was cooling.

"I've been such a jerk, Kyle," Jessica said, reaching over and squeezing his arm. "I'm sorry I've put you through all this. I appreciate you making these arrangements for me and sticking to it. I would have let things go as long as I could, but now, with Charlotte breathing down my neck, you're right. I need everything to be out in the open and cleared up."

"What does Charlotte think she'll find?" Kyle asked, turning on the windshield wipers.

Jessica closed her window and slid over closer to Kyle. "I don't know what she's trying to prove. I haven't done anything illegal or immoral. The bottom line is that I ran away from home. That's it in a nutshell. I'm a twenty-five-year-old run-away. There's no law against that, is there?"

"Why didn't you want anyone to find you?"

Jessica searched her brain for words that she felt comfortable giving to Kyle. "The only way I can say it is that I don't want to be daddy's little girl anymore. I know that probably doesn't make sense to you, Kyle, but it's the best explanation I can offer you right now. Maybe when I come back Sunday night I can clarify things for you. For now, all I can tell you is that if I ever hoped to have my own life, it had to be far away from my father."

"How are things different now?" Kyle asked.

"Nothing is different," Jessica said quickly, resting her hand on top of his. "Except me. I'm different. In all the bizarre circumstances I've been through in the past few months, I think I've changed a lot. I believe I can stand up to my father now and tell him I've made my own life and I intend to live it without his intervention. He will be angry when I tell him I've become a Christian."

"Why's that?"

"Let's just say Christianity doesn't mix well with my father's lifestyle."

"Are you going to be okay?" Kyle asked. "Do you want me to go with you?"

Jessica gave his shoulder a squeeze. "I'll be okay. Thanks for asking, though. And really, Kyle, thanks for making me do this. I can't believe how much lighter I feel inside knowing that I'm going to clear up this whole mess. You were right when you said that a secret is a heavy thing to carry around. Thank you, Kyle, for cutting my burden in half."

Kyle glanced at Jessica and said, "Jess, I'm not even sure I know what your secret is. But I guess I don't need to know all the details. It's enough for me to see you're willing to make room in your life for me." He slipped his arm around her shoulder and said, "Funny thing about hearts. They can be as big as the ocean. But there's only room in them to either be open or to harbor secrets. My heart's open, Jess. It's waiting for you. But I refuse to share your heart with an unresolved secret."

Jessica basked in the honesty of Kyle's words.

"This is a housecleaning weekend," Jessica said. "Or should I say heart-cleaning. I promise you, Kyle, when I return, everything will be in order and ready for you to move in."

He leaned over and kissed her softly on the temple. "That's what I've been praying for," he said.

Chapter Twenty-One

Jessica felt lighthearted during the flight to Los Angeles. She was able to catch an earlier flight and arrived in the early afternoon. As she stood in line at Hertz to pick up the car Kyle had rented for her, Jessica thought of how giving Kyle was. He had made all these arrangements for her, and when she said she would pay him back, he had brushed aside the offer as if the gift were of several dollars rather than several hundred. He had reserved an economy car for her, but Jessica asked for an upgrade. "A convertible please," she said, pulling out her Oregon driver's license.

The autumn afternoon was clear and sunny. Not too much smog and just enough of a breeze to keep things cool. The change was welcome from the drizzle they had experienced in Oregon for the past week and a half. Jessica pulled the red convertible onto the freeway and moved over to the fast lane as quickly as she could. The traffic was light and so was Jessica's mood when she turned off on Sunset Boulevard and drove the familiar streets.

She thought about making a quick detour down to Venice Beach but realized she needed to face her father first. She could play on Saturday. Maybe she would go out to brunch at Chez Monique's in Santa Monica. Or go shopping at the Beverly Center for some new boots to brace her for the Oregon slush she would return to.

Jessica made a left-hand turn into a residential area and wound up the hill. She pulled up to the white, locked gates and pressed her security code into the box beside her car. "Dennis?" She spoke into the box. "Are you there, Dennis?"

"Jessica?" came the startled voice, crackling through the box.

"Yes, it's me. Surprise! Can you let me in?"

"Yes, ma'am!" The tall, ornate gates electronically swung open, and Jessica roared through them, around the fountain, and stopped in front of a uniformed man at the entryway to the lavish mansion.

"Dennis," Jessica said, laughing as she hopped out and gave the man her keys and a big hug. "You look like a fish!" He was opening and closing his mouth, with his eyes bulging, but no sounds came from him.

"Where have you been?" Dennis asked when he found his voice. "Does your father know you're here?"

"Not yet," Jessica said, giving Dennis a quick peck on the cheek. "It's good to see you."

She stepped up to the front door. Before she could turn the knob, the door opened, and Elsie, one of the servants, curtsied and said, "Welcome home, Miss Jessica. We've all missed you."

Jessica hugged Elsie, as well as three other servants who suddenly appeared. They were all too well trained to fully show their emotional shock, and they knew better than to ask her any questions.

"Is my father home?"

Elsie nodded. "He just walked in a few minutes ago. I'm surprised you didn't pass each other on the freeway."

"We might have," Jessica said, feeling her heart beat a little faster. She was ready for this, wasn't she? "I'll see you later." She gave them all a smile and headed for her father's office in the south wing.

Jessica couldn't help but notice how immaculate and expensive everything was. She hadn't paid attention to the luxuries that had surrounded her when she was growing up here. Now, in contrast to her little cottage, everything seemed spacious and ornate. She hated it.

Slipping quietly into her father's office, Jessica saw that Sharon was on the phone, taking notes, with her head down. She didn't notice Jessica.

"Yes," Sharon said, "I do remember you calling earlier. Yes, Mr. Morgan is in the office. Let me put him on the line for you." Sharon pressed a button, still not looking up or noticing Jessica. "Mr. Morgan? The woman I told you about, a Ms. Mendelson, is on line one." Sharon saw Jessica; the secretary looked as if she might faint.

Jessica pressed her finger to her lips. "Let me surprise him," she said.

Without a word, Sharon pushed the security button on her desk to release the lock on the office door. Jessica tiptoed in. Her father was hunched over the desk, barking into the speakerphone. "Yes, yes. You're a school principal. Now where is my daughter?"

"Right here, Daddy," Jessica said. She stood her ground and watched her father's head snap up and his mouth drop open.

"Are you still there, Mr. Morgan?" Charlotte's voice crackled over the speakerphone. "Mr. Morgan?"

Jessica stepped forward and said, "Yes, Charlotte, he's here. And so am I." Jessica pressed the button on the phone to disconnect the call. Her father rose from his leather chair like a huge bull, fists clenched, knuckles white on the desktop. He stared at her, at her shortened hair, at the scar on her lip. He hoarsely whispered, "Jessica?"

Then, before she could respond with her premeditated hug and kiss, he bellowed, "Where in the world have you been?"

"In Oregon," she answered, trying to remain calm. "We need to talk, Dad."

"We need to do more than talk, Jessica." He stumbled from behind his desk and grabbed her firmly by the shoulders. "Do you have *any* idea what you have put me through? How could you do this to me? What were you thinking? And what on earth are you doing in Oregon?" Depleted of his initial burst of fury, Harold Morgan embraced his only daughter, pressing her face tightly against his suit. With his fierce embrace, Jessica caught the faint scent of whiskey and expensive cigars.

Her father released Jessica and held her at arm's length. Had his thick, dark hair gone grayer around the temples? Perhaps his stylist was trying a new look on him. It seemed to her that he had had a chin tuck. Or else he had lost some weight. He wasn't much taller than Jessica, but Harold Morgan was a thick man who devoted an hour a day to disciplined exercise with his personal trainer to keep his 198 pounds from tipping over the 200 mark.

"What happened to your lip?"

"I was in a slight accident. It wasn't a big deal." Jessica hated the way he was checking her out, looking her over for blemishes as if she were a fine bred racing horse. She felt the familiar walls of being owned closing in on her.

"Sharon!" Harold called out. The double doors opened.

"Yes, Mr. Morgan?"

"Sharon, get Nate Goldberg on the phone and schedule Jessie for cosmetic first thing Monday morning. Then call Greg and—"

"Mr. Fletcher is on his way over," Sharon assured him. "And I've reached all the board members except Peter to inform them of the emergency meeting at seven o'clock tonight. Will there be anything else?"

"Not now. Just make sure you get ahold of Peter. And where's the meeting? Downtown?"

"No, I scheduled it for here, sir. Would you like me to change it?"

"Dad," Jessica tried to cut in.

He waved her to keep silent.

"No, no. Here is good. Have the staff prepare the hearth-side room. Seven o'clock, then. Send Greg in here when he arrives."

Sharon nodded and left, closing the doors behind her.

"Dad, I'm not coming to the board meeting. Not tonight. Not ever. That's why we need to talk. I'm declining my position on the board. I don't want anything to do with the corporation. I'm a teacher. I'm happy, and that's what I want to do with my life." Jessica spoke fast, knowing he would bombard her with rebuttals and accusations the instant she stopped to catch her breath. It shocked her that he didn't say a word.

"Come, sit down." He motioned to the couch, his voice smooth as butter.

Jessica refused to sit down, refused to have her father soft-glove her the way she had seen him smoothly handle dozens of clients right before he moved in to close the deal.

"You don't mind if I sit down, do you? It's not every day a man's daughter walks in his office after she's been missing for fifty-four days. Fifty-four of the longest days of a man's life, during which time he receives no word. No hope. Nothing to give him a shred of confidence his daughter is even alive.

"No word at all," he continued, "except this." He pulled from his pocket a well-worn piece of Jessica's letterhead.

"Dear Father," he read, "I've come to the conclusion that as long as I am under your roof, I will never become my own person. Please try to understand. I'm not doing this to hurt you." He looked up, finishing the letter from memory. "I have to do this for myself. Please don't try to find me. Love, Jessica." He walked back to the couch and sat down. He looked at her with what may have been hurt in his eyes. Jessica wasn't sure; she had never seen that expression on his face before.

"Dad, I need you to understand. What I said in that note is true. As long as I'm under your roof, I'll always be your little girl. I'll never be able to think for myself or stretch or become the person I want to be." Jessica lowered herself onto the couch next to her dad. She wanted to take his hand in hers, but he never had been that kind of father. Even now he sat perfectly straight. "I meant what I said, Dad. I'm not doing this to hurt you. I'm doing this because I need to do it for me. Is there any way you can understand that?

Her father sat motionless, studying Jessica. "You can have whatever you want here. Why isn't that good enough for you? Why did you mock me by disappearing? I hired private investigators. The best. Week after week they came up empty. Do you have any idea what you've done to me?"

For the first time, she saw her father's point of view, and she felt badly. "I'm sorry, Dad. I didn't think I had any choice. I had to vanish or I wouldn't be strong enough to leave."

"Why? You could have told me you wanted to be a teacher. I would have let you. I agreed to let you go to Oxford, didn't I?"

Jessica shook her head. "Don't you see? I don't want to

spend the rest of my life begging you for freedom and waiting until you 'let' me go where I want to go or do what I want to do. And even at Oxford I didn't have my own life with Ruben following me everywhere I went."

"What was wrong with Ruben? He was the best bodyguard on my staff. I thought you liked him."

"Of course I liked Ruben. What I didn't like was constantly being watched and followed. I knew that as long as I was under your control and your money, there would always be a Ruben or someone to report back to you everything I did. I don't want to live like that. I can't live like that. I needed to start fresh, all by myself. With no one trying to control me."

She waited for his reaction. When he didn't respond, she decided to make certain he understood her position.

"You need to know," Jessica said, gathering her courage, "I'm only here until Sunday. I came back so that you and I, not the board of directors, but you and I, can resolve some outstanding issues. The first is that I choose to remove myself from the board of directors of Morgan Enterprises." She stopped, realizing she didn't sound like a small-town high school English teacher anymore. She had somehow switched into her young heiress jargon, the junior vice president role she had always hated. It scared her to see how quickly it all came back.

"We can talk," Harold said calmly. "First we should have dinner. You might enjoy freshening up a bit. A swim maybe? A massage? The men will only be here for a short time for the board meeting. You might enjoy sitting in for five minutes. That's all. Five minutes."

"Dad, I'm not going to the board meeting. I'm not a child who can be bribed by a swim. Don't you understand what I'm saying?"

"Yes, I understand. You're not a child anymore." His voice grew soft. "You're twenty-five. Time to claim your inheritance.

Go ahead, Jessica, take it and leave. Greg will prepare the papers for you to sign." He looked defeated, not a familiar expression on the strong face of Harold Morgan III. Jessica wanted him to understand so he wouldn't feel as hurt, so he would understand it wasn't a betrayal of him, but a discovery of who she was.

"I don't want the money. I left here with nothing. Didn't you notice that? I took less than three hundred dollars with me when I left. That's all. I've managed to live for nearly two months on almost nothing! I actually went a couple of days without food because I had no money. Dad, I don't even have a car. And I'm so happy."

Harold looked at Jessica with his brows furrowed. "How could you possibly be happy? You're talking nonsense. And why go without food when you have at your fingertips all the money you could ever want? And you haven't stopped to think about how all this has affected me. I've been miserable. Absolutely out of my mind miserable!"

"Dad, I am sorry I've hurt you. But I'm living the kind of life Mom had while she was growing up. I hang my clothes on the line in my backyard, I walk to work each day, and I have a garden. You know so little about me, about who I really am. If you did, you would know this is all I ever wanted. I've never been happier. And Dad, there's one other thing."

Harold Morgan shrugged his shoulders as if he couldn't even begin to guess what other ridiculous conclusion his daughter had come to.

"I've become a Christian. One of those born-again kind." A smile spread across Jessica's face. "And I met a man who doesn't know a thing about the money, and he loves me for me. Just for who I am. Can you imagine that?"

Harold looked at Jessica as if he had never seen her before in his life. "You're talking like a crazy woman. What did you do? Get kidnapped by some maniacal cult and let them brain-wash you? They have a leader, don't they? He sent you here to get my money. That's what it is, isn't it?"

The office doors burst open, and her father's fifty-two-year-old, energetic lawyer charged into the room, complete with briefcase and paisley necktie. "Jessica!" He dropped the brief-case and opened his arms to receive her embrace.

He had adored her since she was a child. Jessica had learned to go to Greg Fletcher for hugs rather than to her father. If she had been the promiscuous type, she probably would have had an affair with Greg when she was in college. However, nothing of the sort ever happened, and she still thought of herself as a niece to Greg.

A long-distance runner, Greg's trim physique was offset by a shock of pure white hair, which he wore neatly trimmed in the front and in a three-inch ponytail in the back.

"Jessica," Greg let go and then impulsively hugged her again. "You're back!" She caught the brief scent of cinnamon chewing gum on his breath, and suddenly she knew why she had felt so comforted smelling that scent on Kyle. Greg had been the only person in the corporation she had ever felt safe around. He was a man of integrity. Quite a rare thing in Beverly Hills and even more rare in Morgan Enterprises, her father's electronics corporation.

"Let's kill the fatted calf!" Greg said enthusiastically, lifting both his arms in the air. "The prodigal daughter has returned!"

Chapter Twenty-Two

essica lounged on the sofa in the middle of her old bed-room. A fire blazed in the corner fireplace, which had been added several years ago and was more ornamental than ser-viceable. She sat with her feet tucked under her, wearing a plush white robe and rabbit-fur scuffs. On the antique coffee table in front of her was laid out a full English tea, complete with currant scones, Devonshire cream, fresh strawberries, and cucumber sandwiches. The servant had poured Jessica a cup of tea, added cream and one lump of sugar, then left it for Jessica on the silver tray. And there it sat, getting cold.

She had called down for the tea because she wanted to eat something before driving back to the airport in an hour. Yet she couldn't bring herself to touch any of it. Her mind was glutted with the events of the past two days. Jessica wished she could somehow pull a big plug and let all the information drain out through a strainer so she might save the really important things and let the rest go.

Someone knocked on her bedroom door. Jessica called out, "Come in."

Greg entered and closed the door. "Tea time?" he asked cheerfully.

"Please help yourself," Jessica offered. "I can't quite manage to eat anything."

Greg reached for a cucumber sandwich and popped the triangular morsel into his mouth. He settled himself in one of the plush wing back chairs and said, "So, you haven't changed your mind?"

"No, I haven't changed my mind."

"Will you miss your home here?" Greg asked, pouring himself a cup of tea from the elegant silver pot.

"I didn't before," Jessica said. "When I was in Glenbrooke these past few months, that was my life and all this," she motioned to the ornately decorated room filled with priceless antique furniture and designer linens, "was a fairy tale."

"The princess leaves the castle and never looks back," Greg quipped. He had on a pair of shorts, running shoes, and white T-shirt, looking like a track runner who had triumphantly broken the ribbon. He certainly didn't look his fifty-two years.

"Only I looked back," Jessica said.

"And you're afraid that now you'll turn into a pillar of salt and blow away."

"What?"

"You know," Greg said, "Lot's wife. Sodom and Gomorrah. She looked back when she was supposed to flee, and she turned into a pillar of salt. Never mind. Do you want some fresh tea? This is cold."

"Sure," Jessica said. "Go ahead and ring for it. I'm going to get dressed." She retreated to her bathroom with the sunken spa tub, exercise bicycle, tanning bed, and fresh flower arrangement on the counter. The contrast to her little bathroom in Glenbrooke, with the claw-foot tub, window with no screen, and chipped paint on the windowsill, was sharp. Only an hour earlier Jessica had emerged from the indoor pool and received a forty-minute massage and a facial. Now she stood in front of a half dozen mirrors and slipped her pampered body into a new sweater and the same pair of jeans she had worn all night in Mexico when the truck was stuck in the mud. The contrasts were a bit overwhelming.

Jessica felt she had done a pretty good job of keeping her perspective during the weekend. She had engaged in heated discussions with her father; negotiated with several of the older, more hard-nosed board members; and even maneuvered her way through a last-ditch effort from Peter, the head of their German division, to change her mind. Peter had taken her to dinner last night, and in the middle of their baked Alaska had proposed to her. When she turned him down, he said, "Your father will be disappointed. He said I was his final hope for keeping you in the corporation. Not that he was the only reason I proposed. I think you would make a fine wife."

Greg had been the only clear-headed advisor throughout the weekend, and she had relied heavily on him.

With one last look in the multiple mirrors, she left her bathroom forever and felt glad that her little home in Glenbrooke had only one full-length mirror—and that was on the downstairs coat closet door. Too many mirrors, like too much self-evaluation, can lead to bitter discouragement. Jessica knew this only too well.

"You haven't told me what you think," Jessica said, joining Greg and one of the girls from the kitchen staff who had just brought in a fresh pot of tea. "Thank you," Jessica said to the slender woman. "Do you want something to eat? Some strawberries perhaps?"

The girl looked startled at Jessica's suggestion and politely declined, leaving the room like a spooked rabbit.

"Really, Jessica," Greg said, pouring fresh cups of tea, "inviting the kitchen staff to join you in your room for some refreshment! You have changed, my girl." He handed the china cup and saucer to Jessica. "And I, for one, think it's wonderful. You've made some monumental decisions this weekend. I believe they'll all be for your ultimate best. But then, I'm your lawyer. I'm supposed to tell you positive things like that."

"So what you're saying is that you don't really think I'm making the right choice."

"I didn't say that. I'm just saying that I don't know of any other woman who, given your situation, would make the choices you've made."

"Greg, please tell me you understand why I have to walk away from this."

Greg didn't answer. He tilted his head and waited for her to explain. "To me, this is all a prison, a beautiful, luxurious confinement. Greg, do you remember ever hearing my mother talk about when she was a girl and she made applesauce from the apples off a tree?"

Greg shook his head and sipped his steaming cup of tea.

"Something inside me needs to do that."

"Make applesauce?"

"Yes, make applesauce. Don't you see? This prison is so confining, I can't walk into the kitchen and do whatever I want. The kitchen help would order me to leave, or they would take over and make it for me. This lifestyle doesn't match who I really am."

Jessica sat back, not sure if she would ever be able to express to Greg or to anyone why she so desperately desired the kind of life Glenbrooke offered her. Maybe she was hoping to forge some emotional connection with her mother and the simple life she had known before she had married Harold

Morgan. Maybe Jessica's longing to escape the imprisoning way her father had ruled her life pushed her into the decision. Or maybe the choice to leave stemmed from the fear she had harbored that no man would ever love her for who she was rather than for what she possessed as long as she associated herself with her father's enterprises and finances. Probably all of those motivations—and others that she couldn't even express to herself—had urged her on.

"Then Jessica, for you, for right now, this is a good decision." Greg interrupted her reverie. "As a matter of fact, as your friend, not your lawyer, but as your friend, I applaud you. Especially for your decision to make Christ the center of your life. That was my childhood training, you know. And in the past year, I feel that's what I'm returning to. It seems as if God has been rather obstinate about bringing me back into the fold."

"He is pretty relentless, isn't he?"

Greg tipped his cup of tea toward her in a toast of agreement and took a sip. Placing the cup back on the saucer, he said, "Now. How about those papers we have for you to sign?" He fished out the stack of legal papers from his briefcase.

"Sign at the bottom of each page, Jess. That's right. And this one, and this one, and two places to sign on this one. Wait, did you initial page six? Yes, okay. Good. Only a few more. And there you go!" Greg straightened the stack of documents and placed them back in his briefcase. "There. That wasn't so bad now, was it?"

Jessica smiled and reached for a strawberry. "I guess not."

"You have all the documents I gave you this morning?"

"Yes, in my purse."

"You're all set then." Greg stood up and opened his arms, welcoming Jessica into his friendly hug one last time. She rose and hugged him and gave him a kiss on the cheek.

"Thanks, Greg. Really. Thanks for everything."

"You will call me if you need anything, won't you?"

"Of course. Give my love to Holly and the kids."

"I will." Greg looked as if he were fighting back some emotion. "You, Jessica Grace Morgan, are a woman of substance. I'm honored to know you."

He sounded so chivalrous, so final in his good-bye, that it made Jessica feel a bit shaken. It had been one thing to run away in secret two months ago and live in hiding. It was completely different to walk away from all this and have her dad's lawyer send her off with a poetic tossing of the coat over the mud puddle, so to speak.

"Do you need a ride to the airport or are you taking the limo?"

"Actually, Kyle rented a car for me. I need to drive it back to the airport."

"So that's his name," Greg said. "Kyle must be quite a guy."

"He's not like any other man I've ever met. Except maybe for you, Greg." Jessica said it with a wink and then got up and slipped on her shoes. She zipped up her garment bag and looped her purse over her shoulder.

"Let me at least carry that for you," Greg said, picking up the bulging bag. "Good grief! What are you doing, Jess, stealing the family silver?"

"Just a few photos," she said. "I asked dad."

"You said your good-byes with him already?"

"Yes." Jessica snagged one last strawberry and took one last sweeping glance at her old room before following Greg out the door. "We had a long talk this afternoon. I apologized for the way I left two months ago. At the time, I couldn't think of any other way to break free from the leash he had on my life. No, I'm leaving openly and with everything in order. But he still won't give me his blessing. To my dad, there's only one way, and that's his way. I can't live like that. Or should I say, I won't live like that."

Greg led her down the wide, sweeping staircase to the main entryway. All the staff were lined up in their neatly pressed black and white uniforms, prepared to say farewell to Jessica. She said good-bye to each of them and waved again from the front seat of her rental car before pulling out of the driveway.

She thought of how no one had noticed her early morning departure the last time she had left. Glancing in her rearview mirror, she noticed a solitary figure standing at the window of her father's upstairs bedroom. Jessica bit her lip and whispered, "Good-bye, Daddy. Please, please try to understand."

The autumn wind whipped Jessica's hair as she drove to the airport. To get her mind off her dad, she thought about Kyle and how she would explain all this to him. He might not believe her.

She could always have Greg call him, and he could tell Kyle the truth—that Jessica Morgan was the daughter of a multi-millionaire and of her own free will, she chose to step down from the vice president position of Morgan Enterprises, a position which legally became hers on her twenty-fifth birthday.

Jessica played over a dozen other scenarios in her exhausted mind during the flight back to Portland. What if Charlotte had found a way to fire her? Or what if the school board sided with Charlotte and agreed Jessica was out of line in asking Kyle to be a guest speaker without first sending home a letter to the parents? It occurred to Jessica that she might have resigned as vice president only to find herself fired from her teaching job.

The plane landed at midnight, and Jessica entered the terminal, eager to see Kyle. There he stood, waiting for her with a bouquet of mixed flowers in his hand. Jessica walked right into his arms.

"Welcome home," Kyle said, holding her close. "I missed you."

"I missed you, too," Jessica said, her cheek pressed against his chest.

"How did everything go?" Kyle handed her the flowers, and looping his arm around her shoulders, he started walking with her toward the baggage claim.

"It went about the way I thought it would."

"And is that good?" Kyle asked.

"Yes, I think it turned out well." Jessica realized she could hardly give Kyle a straight answer when he was unaware of any of the details of her situation. She thought of what a trusting man he was to send her on this journey, not knowing what issues she was trying to resolve.

As soon as they were in his truck headed back to Glenbrooke, Jessica started to fill in the details for him. "I talked a lot with my dad. He's not very much in favor of my staying here, or of my choosing teaching as my career. I don't know if he'll ever fully understand or support me, but I know this is the best thing for me."

"Good," Kyle said. "I think your staying in Glenbrooke is the best thing, too. But then, I have my personal reasons." He turned to Jessica and winked.

"My relationship with my father has always been distant and strained," she continued. "I didn't expect him to respond any differently from how he has in the past."

"It must have made it hard then to trust God," Kyle said.

"Why do you say that?"

"I think we tend to view our heavenly Father the same way we view our earthly fathers. He's not like that at all, you know. God, I mean. He's loving, forgiving, and merciful toward us. There's nothing we can ever do to make him stop loving us. All he wants is for us to trust him and love him. That's where it becomes hard when our human fathers aren't trustworthy or loving."

Jessica thought of her dad's aloofness and his fierce anger. Kyle had a point. That *was* how she had pictured God. Until last week, that is.

Then Jessica had another thought. Kyle would make an incredible father. *I wonder how many children he wants?*

She shook herself out of the future and back to the present. "I'm glad you urged me to face him, Kyle. I don't know why I thought I could let things continue in limbo, the way they were. I needed to go back, just like you said, and make some decisions and set a few things in order. Thanks for making me go."

"Then I suppose I should thank you for making me bring my secret about Lindsey's death out in the open. This morning at church, four different sets of parents came up to me and said their kids came home and told them about my speaking in your class."

"Uh-oh. Were they upset about not receiving letters?"

"Not at all. They said it was the first time they were able to sit down with their teens and talk openly about sex. Their kids had decided in your class that the only way for them was abstinence."

"Kyle, that's great! I hope the school board hears about it."

Kyle smiled. "They have. Three of the parents I spoke to are on the school board, and one of them just happens to be superintendent of schools."

"You're kidding!"

"Nope. Oh, one other thing. It just so happens that there's one school board member I don't think Charlotte intended to have to deal with. It'll be pretty tough trying to convince this board member that you should be reprimanded for your actions."

"Who is it?"

"Me."

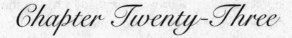

Chapter Twenty-Three

*K*yle and Jessica arrived back at her home at about two-thirty in the morning. They had spent most of the trip from the airport discussing the situation at school with Charlotte. The school board meeting was scheduled for that night, and Kyle coached Jessica on how to present her position when and if the board called on her.

They had become so caught up with the Charlotte problem that Jessica hadn't filled Kyle in on some of the vital information she had planned to tell him. He parked the truck, carried in her luggage, and was about to go when she said, "I wanted to give you this." Jessica filed through the papers in her purse until she came to a check written out to Kyle.

When he saw the check, he put up both his hands and said, "I don't want you to pay me back for the plane ticket."

"Then take this as gas money for the ride to the airport and back." She held out the check to him, but he still refused to take it.

"Kyle, please take it. For two months I've had nothing to give to anyone. Please accept this from me. It's offered from my heart."

Kyle smiled at her and accepted the check. He casually glanced at it before he began to stuff it in his pocket. Then he did a double take and burst out laughing.

"That's what I enjoy about you," Kyle said, waving the check in the air, "your great sense of humor. Five hundred thousand dollars! That's a good one, Jess."

Jessica's facial expression didn't change.

"What?" Kyle said. He seemed to be trying to read her serious look. "Did I miss something? Was it supposed to be one of those coupons good for half a million hugs or something?" He studied the check, then looked up with a punchy expression on his face.

"It's good, Kyle."

"What do you mean it's good? You're saying I could take this to the bank tomorrow and cash it?"

"No, you could deposit it. Banks don't usually give out more than ten thousand in cash."

Kyle looked confused and as though he were about to burst out laughing at the same time.

"I haven't told you something important," Jessica said. "Besides my father being aloof and all that, he's also a millionaire. A multi-millionaire, to be exact."

Kyle sobered.

"When I turned twenty-five last month, my trust fund became available to me, and I was automatically given the position of vice president of Morgan Enterprises."

"As in Morgan Electronics?" Kyle said, his face turning pale.

Jessica nodded. "That's what I was running away from. I

wanted a new life away from my dominating father and his money and all the cutthroat negotiating I'd grown up with. I felt imprisoned by the power and the money and the lifestyle. Starting over with a new identity was the only way I thought I could leave all that behind. You showed me I could come out of hiding, face my responsibilities, and then legally walk away from them."

Kyle sat down hard on the bottom step, staring at the check.

"I resigned my position," Jessica said, sitting down next to him. "I had to sign over my trust fund to the corporation. But my dad's lawyer found a way I could come away with some money by selling my shares of the company. I basically cashed out. I'm free to live my life the way I want. Or maybe I should say, the way God wants me to."

Kyle looked at Jessica, his eyes still wide with disbelief. "I can't take this," he said hoarsely.

"Of course you can!" Jessica felt relieved to finally let out her secret. "You're holding a check in your hand that's good for half a million dollars. You said that's all you needed. Only a half a million. You can build your orphanage now." She tried to make contact through his glazed eyes with the man inside. "Or start your fund to send kids to college." Jessica waved a hand in front of his vacant expression. "Hello in there!"

Kyle didn't respond.

"It's not that much, Kyle. I have more than $47 million, so don't feel as if you're cutting into my profit or anything."

He still sat stupefied.

Jessica tried to think of something to make him laugh. "I know, what about Kenya? We could try to buy Kenya, if you still wanted to."

Kyle shot up as if he had been electrocuted. His arm

snapped toward Jessica, and he held the check as far away from him as he could. "I can't take this!" he said, sounding frantic. "I don't want your money!"

When Jessica wouldn't take it back, Kyle ripped the check into a dozen pieces and tossed it at her. Without saying a word, he left.

She was stunned. She'd never expected this kind of reaction from him. All her life men had chased her because of her money. She never knew if any of them were sincerely interested in her or only in what they would gain by marrying her. Kyle was the opposite of those other men, yet she'd never expected him to reject her because of her money. The thought that she had lost him came as a sharp and bitter blow.

"I don't know what I was thinking he would say," Jessica said to Teri after school the next day. When Teri drove her home as usual, Jessica had invited her in for a soda and cautiously proceeded to confide in her. "The people in this town are the first people in my whole life who have treated me normally, like an average person. But now I'm starting to think I really am a sort of freak. I don't want people to know about the money if it means everyone is going to change around me. I feel as if I'm losing everything I desperately desired to have here in Glenbrooke. Teri, it's awful."

Teri blew a long breath of air out through her mouth. A funny, clown-like smile lit up her face. "Yeah, I bet it's awful."

"It is. You don't understand. People think all their problems would be solved if they had a million dollars. Well, I do, and they're not. I only have more problems. Complex problems."

Teri looked as if she were trying her best to understand. Jessica reached across the couch and squeezed Teri's arm. "Will you still be my friend? I'm not good at making friends because I've always been kind of isolated. Ingrown. This is so pathetic, but I can honestly say that you are the first true friend I've ever had. Except for maybe Greg, my dad's lawyer."

A look of recognition spread across Teri's face. "Greg Fletcher? That man who called here awhile back?"

Jessica nodded.

"No wonder you looked so rattled when I hung up on him. Oh, Jessica, I can't even begin to imagine what you've gone through. You really were completely out of food the day the groceries came, weren't you?"

Jessica nodded. "I didn't plan my escape very well. I only had twelve dollars to last for about three weeks."

"Oh, Jessica!" Teri reached over and hugged her. "Why didn't you tell me? I would have done anything I could have for you."

"I know," Jessica said. "Actually, could I ask you to do a favor for me now?"

"Sure. Anything."

Jessica went to her secretary and pulled out a torn corner of a grocery store bag. "Do you know a little boy named Adam Kelsey?"

"Sure. He has a cousin, Laura, in one of my classes."

"Could you see that he somehow gets this, anonymously?" Jessica handed Teri a hundred dollar bill. "One day at the grocery store, when I used the last of my twelve dollars and came up a nickel short, this little angel gave me one of his pop can nickels. I promised I'd pay him back."

Teri took the money and a mischievous look crossed her face. "You know what? Nobody around here needs to know about the money, unless Kyle says anything, which I doubt he would. You said you wanted to use it to help people. We could set it up so that you can give to your heart's content and nobody would know where it was coming from."

"I like it," Jessica said, feeling relieved that Teri was warming up to the idea of Jessica being a millionaire.

"And don't worry about Kyle. I think he'll come around once the shock wears off. He fell in love with you hard and fast when he thought you were a poverty case. He loves you, not your money."

Jessica felt encouraged by Teri's words and hoped with everything inside her that Teri was right. Tonight at the school board meeting Jessica would find out.

Teri suggested they run over to the Wallflower for dinner before going to the meeting. Jessica ordered a bowl of soup and sipped at it, barely tasting the beef and vegetables. She was nervous about seeing Kyle and being prepared for the accusations that would come at her from Charlotte.

Teri chatted on about her sister in Hawaii and wolfed down a tuna melt and cottage fries. When the bill came, Jessica reached for it before Teri could and said, "You paid last time. I have this one covered."

Teri started to laugh. She laughed until she had tears in her eyes and was holding onto her side. People were looking at them, and still Teri couldn't stop laughing.

"What's so funny?" Jessica leaned forward and tried to get Teri to come back to earth.

"You said," Teri gasped for air, "you said you had this one covered."

"Right. What's so funny about that?"

Teri broke into another spasm, trying to swallow the laughter. She waved her hand in front of her face, fanning herself. "I'm sorry, Jess. It's just that when you said that, I realized you could pay for dinner for everyone in this restaurant." She kept her voice low and leaned forward with her eyes glistening. "You could cover this whole town—the whole state of Oregon—and still have money left over."

Jessica didn't understand why that was so funny and tried her best to force a smile.

"I'm sorry," Teri said, calming down. "I'm sorry. It's just a shock when you think about it. It's not really funny, I guess."

Teri composed herself and apologized again on the way to the school. "I don't know why I reacted like that. I hope I did-n't embarrass you."

"No, that's okay. Don't worry about it." Jessica didn't under-stand. However, it did make her wonder if Kyle's reaction stemmed from the same kind of emotional well that Teri had drawn from tonight. The expectations that had been placed on Jessica and her inheritance money for so many years had cre-ated a wealth of painful feelings in her. All she'd ever wanted was a simple life. Now that she had it, she was trying to think of how the people around her would respond to her suddenly having all this money. If she had kept her position as vice pres-ident, her assets would have been more than four hundred mil-lion, and when her father died, it would have all been hers. So what? She had more than she needed, and she had the life she wanted. Now, if she could only be sure she had Kyle.

The meeting began on time, and Jessica watched Kyle care-fully from where she and Teri sat toward the back of the room. She was certain that he had noticed her when she walked in, but Kyle wouldn't make eye contact with her. It made her nervous.

About ten minutes into the meeting, Dawn and her father, Dr. Laughlin, slipped into the back of the room. A few more of Jessica's students and their parents entered the room. By the time the agenda reached item six, "Ms. Morgan-Fenton: Violation of Parental Notification," all the seats at the back of the room were filled with parents and students. Jessica hoped these were the supportive ones Kyle had mentioned. Or they might be a gathering of those who had complained to Charlotte.

Charlotte seemed to delight in describing the way Jessica had let a guest speaker in her class without first clearing it and how that speaker had discussed AIDS, without the parents receiving notice ahead of time.

"I also must add that this particular teacher has been in continual violation of a number of district policies," Charlotte continued. "Her files are not complete, even after repeated requests. She went to great lengths to deceive the school district regarding her identity. I was concerned about her blatant lies, such as masquerading under the false name of Fenton, when her real last name was Morgan."

A faint whispering spread across the room. Jessica couldn't deny any of Charlotte's accusations. She had been deceitful. It hadn't bothered Jessica in the beginning, since she felt the end would justify the means for her false identity. Now she felt sick to her stomach over it. Perhaps growing closer to the Lord made the truth more apparent to her. She felt as if she had stepped out of the shadows into the light and found all kinds of flaws blaring in the light that were invisible in the shadows.

She wouldn't blame Kyle for giving up on her. Not because of the shock of the money, but because of all the deception. He didn't even know who she was. Not the real Jessica. An aching fear burned inside her heart when she thought it was possible— no, probable—that Kyle would feel too jerked around to invest any more in a relationship with her.

"I did some checking, since Mr. McGregor apparently didn't, and I found that this woman, Jessica Morgan, is actually the daughter of Harold Morgan. Yes," Charlotte said, nodding to the people around the room who happened to recognize the name, "*the* Harold Morgan, multi-millionaire."

"Well," Teri whispered, "there goes our plan to keep the money a secret."

"Ms. Morgan, will you come to the front?" Charlotte made the statement sound more like a command than a request. A month ago, Jessica would have refused. Tonight, all she could think of was that word that had become so familiar in her sub-conscious, *surrender.*

Jessica stood and walked to the front. She wished she had worn her blue Liz Claiborne suit.

"My question," Charlotte said, pointing her finger at Jessica as she took a seat on the podium behind Charlotte, "is why should we keep such a woman on staff at Glenbrooke High? She lied her way into this position, and the bottom line is that she doesn't need it. I recommend we let this impostor go immediately."

Charlotte's argument was weak; Jessica knew that. No rea-sonable basis existed to fire her. However, this was a small town and a close knit group of school board members. Charlotte Mendelson stood before them with fire in her eyes.

Several people began to speak at once. Charlotte stepped back, and the director of the board rose and called for the room to come to order. One woman in the back remained standing and called out, "She's the best teacher my son has ever had! You can't fire someone because of the color of their skin, and you certainly can't fire them because their father happens to have a lot of money."

"That's right," someone else agreed.

"But she talked to my daughter about AIDS in her class," a woman in a simple blue dress said without standing up. "And she didn't ask my permission!"

"Okay, okay," the director said, raising his hands. "Before this becomes a free-for-all, I have a few things to say. First, Miss Morgan should have sent a notice home, but she didn't. This is her first year, and I believe we can extend some grace to her since she didn't know the policy."

Charlotte spoke up. "She *did* know the policy. I went over it in my meetings before school opened."

"We can overlook the error. And the board doesn't consider any of the other charges serious enough to warrant her removal."

Just then Kyle stepped up to the podium. The director leaned over, and Kyle spoke to him quietly. "Mr. Buchanan now has the floor."

Jessica's heart took an express elevator up to her throat and stopped with a sudden jerk. If anyone could convince the mob one way or the other, it would be Kyle. She wished she knew where she stood with him. If only he would at least *look* at her, she could judge by his expression what he was feeling.

"I'd like to make it clear that Miss Morgan did in fact invite me to be a guest speaker in her class, and I accept all responsibility for the content of my presentation."

"Kyle!" Charlotte's hand flew to her chest. She must not have known who the guest speaker was. The new information seemed to take all the wind out of her sails.

"Also," Kyle continued, "I agree with Mrs. Powell in that a person cannot be discriminated against because of her financial status. I know it's an unusual thing in our town to be acquainted with someone from an affluent background. It's okay if you feel a little startled. I know I was shocked when I found out."

Up until this point, Kyle had been speaking to the audience, with his back to Jessica. Now he turned around and took the four short steps to her chair, reached for her hands, and lifted her to a standing position with his back to the audience.

When she looked into his eyes, Jessica felt a calm flowing over her.

"I'm sorry," Kyle said. "Will you forgive me for being obstinate and insensitive?"

"Of course," Jessica whispered back. "Will you forgive me for not being honest with you? I want to start all over." A runaway tear broke loose and careened down her cheek.

Kyle nodded, and placing his hand on her chin, he wiped away the tear. His finger then found its way to the half-moon on her lip. His green eyes scanned her face. They rested on her lips. Everything within her desired Kyle to kiss her. She didn't care that half the population of Glenbrooke was ogling them.

The director stepped to the microphone again and said, "Ms. Mendelson, I hope you can see that your insensitive and heavy-handed approach is not favorably looked on by the school board. I recommend that you focus your attention on the education of Glenbrooke's teenagers rather than worrying over the files of your teachers."

Charlotte rose and looked over at Kyle and Jessica. Instead of anger, her face bore a pitiable expression.

"And," the director continued, "I suggest we all try to start afresh."

"Maybe I did overstep my boundaries a bit. I trust the school board will overlook that and view my performance in a broader scope." Charlotte seemed to be working hard to exit with her dignity intact. She stepped down from the platform and took a seat toward the back of the room.

"We can start over, too," Kyle said to Jessica. "Do you remember my promise in Mexico?"

Jessica shook her head, her eyes locked on his.

"I promised you that if I ever had a million dollars, I'd buy you a house and plant you a purple hydrangea bush."

"Two hydrangeas," Jessica reminded him, a smile creeping up her mouth, tilting the half-moon toward him.

Kyle leaned down and kissed her hard and long.

Everyone in the room stood up and gave a standing ovation. Even Martin the Masher was clapping. Teri looked jubilant. Kyle wrapped his arm around Jessica's shoulders, and they turned to face the crowd. Kyle gave a playful bow to the audience while Jessica watched as Charlotte rose from her seat, and Mr. Porter, the slightly overweight football coach, discretely followed her out of the room.

"I'm not sure if they're applauding for us or because of how everything turned out with Charlotte and the school board's decision," Jessica said.

Kyle looked down at her. "It's for us, Jess. Half these people have been praying for me for the past four years. You're their answer to prayer."

"And the money doesn't bother you?" Jessica asked.

Kyle cupped her chin in his hand. "No," he said, "all I ask is that you make me a promise."

"Anything."

"Promise me there will be no more secrets."

"No more secrets," Jessica promised, holding up her right hand like a Scout taking a pledge.

A smile spread across Kyle's face as he said, "Then, since the way I feel about you is no longer a secret, I think I'd better affirm these people's faith in prayer by taking you in my arms and kissing you again."

And he did.

The publisher and author would love to hear your comments about this book. *Please contact us at:* http://fiction.mpbooks.com

Secrets Recipe

The kitchen staff at the Morgan Estates prepared a full English tea for Jessica on the afternoon before she returned to Glenbrooke (pg. 245). The danties served on a silver tray included cucumber sandwiches, fresh strawberries, currant scones, and Devonshire cream.

My tea loving friends and I agree. The "Devonshire cream" available in the states is never as good as the true Devonshire or "clotted cream" we've tasted in England, Scotland, and Ireland. I imagine Jessica missed the Devonshire cream she enjoyed while attending Oxford and the kitchen staff at Morgan Estates did their best to duplicate the delicacy. Their recipe below, "Jessica's Devonshire Cream," comes pretty close.

My thanks go to Loch Grant for his advice on the currant scones. And my daughter Rachel is the resident expert on cucumber sandwiches whenever she and I have a tea party. Her advice has been noted.

Morgan Estates Currant Scones

> Preheat over to 325 degrees
> 1/2 cup butter at room temperature
> 1/4 cup sugar
> 1/2 tsp. salt
> 1-1/2 cups sour cream (don't substitute low-fat sour cream)
> 1-1/2 cups cake flour
> 1-1/2 cups all-purpose flour
> 2 tbsp. baking powder
> 3/4 cup dried currants
> 1 tbsp. grated lemon rind

Blend butter, sugar, salt and sour cream at low speed until mixture is creamy. Mix flours and baking powder in separate bowl. Add currants and lemon rind. Mix gently. Form a well in the center of the dry ingredients. Pour butter mixture into the well. Mix until a soft dough is formed. Place dough on a floured surface and knead a few times. Pat into an 8-inch round circle. Cut dough into 10 equal wedges with floured knife. Place wedges 1-1/2 inches apart on an ungreased cookie sheet. Bake on top rack for 40 to 50 minutes. Scones will be a golden brown color. Let cool before serving with Jessica's Devonshire Cream.

Jessica's Devonshire Cream

> 3 ounces light cream cheese
> 1 tsp. sugar
> 1/4 tsp. vanilla extract
> 1 cup heavy cream, at room temperature

Blend the cream cheese and sugar with an electric mixer until light and fluffy. Add vanilla extract and the heavy cream. Beat on high until stiff peaks form. Cover and refrigerate overnight. Serve chilled in a pretty dish with Morgan Estates Currant Scones.

Tea Time Cucumber Sandwiches

> 2 fresh cucumbers
> 1/2 cup soft cream cheese
> 6-8 slices of fresh bread
> Dash of pepper
> Pinch of parsley flakes

Wash cucumbers and peel leaving a strip of skin between each peel to give them a zebra stripe effect. Slice cucumbers into thin rounds. Cut all crusts from the bread and spread with cream cheese. Add a dash of pepper and a pinch of parsley flakes to each slice before adding sliced cucumbers to half the pieces of bread. Put the other piece of bread on top and cut into little finger sandwiches or use cookie cutters to make heart-and flower-shaped sandwiches. Keep the sandwiches covered before serving to prevent the bread from drying out.

Dear Reader:

Last summer my mom came across my grade school report cards and sent them to me. My husband, Ross, and I laughed when we read the teacher's comment at the end of my first grade year: "Robin has not yet grasped her basic math skills. However, she *has* kept the entire class entertained at rug time with her imaginative stories." So! That's where this passion for storytelling began! (It also explains why I can't balance the check book.)

Ross and I have been in full-time youth ministry for the past seventeen years. While our son and daughter were babies I wrote some articles and some children's books. To my amazement, they were published! Then the girls in our youth group started bugging me to write some books for them, so I wrote a series of twelve books for teens called, *The Christy Miller Series*. The passion for storytelling kept growing.

Secrets is my first adult novel. As with all firstborn, there's a sense of wonder when it finally comes forth. And a sense of delight. I'm delighted that this book is a romance. If I'm going to keep telling stories, then I want to tell romances because, to me, romance is the essence of redemption. Think of a relentless lover pursuing his first love until they are at last united. God is the relentless lover and we are His first love.

Thanks for picking up this book. Being able to share these stories with you is sort of a midlife "rug time." May we spend many of them together. And may this romance nudge you into the arms of the relentless lover who knows the secrets of your heart.

Always,

Robin Jones Gunn

P.S. You are invited to come visit me online at www.robingunn.com

TEA AT GLENBROOKE

- Authored by: *Robin Jones Gunn*
- Artist: *Susan Mink Colclough*

Snuggle into an overstuffed chair, sip your favorite tea, and journey to Glenbrooke…"a quiet place where souls are refreshed." Writing from a tender heart, Robin Jones Gunn transports you to an elegant place of respite, comfort, and serenity—a place you'll never want to leave! Look forward to a joyful reading experience, lavishly illustrated by Susan Mink Colclough, that captures the essence of a peaceful place.

ISBN 1-58860-023-8

THE GLENBROOKE SERIES

by *Robin Jones Gunn*

COME TO GLENBROOKE…

A QUIET PLACE WHERE SOULS ARE REFRESHED

I magine a circle of friends who enter into each other's lives during that poignant season when love comes their way. Imagine the sweetness of having those friends to depend on as the journey into marriage and motherhood begins.

Meet the women of Glenbrooke: Jessica, Teri, Lauren, Alissa, Shelly, Meredith, Leah, and Genevieve. When their lives intersect in this small town, the door to friendship is opened and hearts come in to stay.

Perfectly crafted, heartwarming, and rich in truth, Robin's Glenbrooke novels have delighted half a million readers with their insights and charm. All souls looking to be refreshed are warmly invited to come to Glenbrooke.

SECRETS
Glenbrooke Series #1
Beginning her new life in a small Oregon town, high school English teacher Jessica Morgan tries desperately to hide the details of her past.

1-59052-673-2

WHISPERS
Glenbrooke Series #2
Teri went to Maui hoping to start a relationship with one special man. But romance becomes much more complicated when she finds herself pursued by three.

1-59052-192-7

ECHOES
Glenbrooke Series #3
Lauren Phillips "connects" on the Internet with a man known only as "K.C." Is she willing to risk everything...including another broken heart?

1-59052-193-5

SUNSETS
Glenbrooke Series #4
Alissa loves her new job as a Pasadena travel agent. Will an abrupt meeting with a stranger in an espresso shop leave her feeling that all men are like the one she's been hurt by recently?

1-59052-238-9

CLOUDS
Glenbrooke Series #5
After Shelly Graham and her old boyfriend cross paths in Germany, both must face the truth about their feelings.

1-59052-230-3

WATERFALLS
Glenbrooke Series #6
Meri thinks she's finally met the man of her dreams...until she finds out he's movie star Jacob Wilde, promptly puts her foot in her mouth, and ruins everything.

1-59052-231-1

WOODLANDS
Glenbrooke Series #7
Leah Hudson has the gift of giving, but questions her own motives, and God's purposes, when she meets a man she prays will love her just for herself.

1-59052-237-0

WILDFLOWERS
Glenbrooke Series #8
Genevieve Ahrens has invested lots of time and money in renovating the Wildflowers Café. Now her heart needs the same attention.

1-59052-239-7

SISTERCHICK® Adventures by

ROBIN JONES GUNN

SISTERCHICK *n.*: a friend who shares the deepest wonders of your heart, loves you like a sister, and provides a reality check when you're being a brat.

SISTERCHICKS ON THE LOOSE!

Zany antics abound when best friends Sharon and Penny take off on a midlife adventure to Finland, returning home with a new view of God and a new zest for life.

SISTERCHICKS DO THE HULA!

It'll take more than an unexpected stowaway to keep two middle-aged sisterchicks from reliving their college years with a little Waikiki wackiness—and learning to hula for the first time.

www.sisterchicks.com

SISTERCHICKS IN SOMBREROS

Two Canadian sisters embark on a journey to claim their inheritance—beachfront property in Mexico—not expecting so many bizarre, wacky problems! But they're nothing a little coconut cake can't cure...

SISTERCHICKS DOWN UNDER!

Kathleen meets Jill at the Chocolate Fish café in New Zealand and they instantly forge a friendship. Now Robin Jones Gunn reveals their crazy adventures in classic Sisterchick style!

SISTERCHICKS SAY OOH LA LA!

Painting toenails and making promises under the canopy of a princess bed seals a friendship for life! Over thirty years of ups and downs find Lisa and Amy still Best Friends Forever... and off on an unforgettable Paris rendezvous!

SISTERCHICKS IN GONDOLAS
Available June 2006!

w w w . s i s t e r c h i c k s . c o m

Sisterchicks in Sombreros
Available now!

The last Saturday of November, I stood in the garage untangling a string of twinkle lights and thinking, *Who came up with the term* Father Christmas?

At our house, it's more like *Mother Christmas*. I'm the one who knows where all the decorations are stored. I organize the festivities, buy all the gifts, address all the cards, initiate all the parties, and single-handedly festoon the house. Without the information stored in my brain and the loving labor of my two hands, Christmas would not come to our humble abode in Langley, British Columbia.

I always begin with a long list of what needs to be done and tell myself to start earlier than I did the previous year. Getting the lights untangled on November 29 was a pretty good running start.

That is, until Aunt Winnie called.

The shuttle van pulled off the freeway, and I could see our cruise ship docked and waiting. As we got closer, the ship got larger and larger. Stepping out of the van, I stood beside the others while a porter came along and tagged our baggage. In front of me the ship dominated our view. It was huge. On the top deck, I could see people leaning on the railing. They were so high up.

An unexpected queasy sensation came over me, squeezing my stomach. My courage had sprung a leak, and I was shocked to realize that I was terrified!

What am I doing here? I can't go on that ship. I can't go to Mexico. I don't belong here. I need to go home. Right now.

Perspiration poured down my neck. It took every shred of nerve for me not to let out a shriek and go running after the airport shuttle as it began to pull away. I'd never had a reaction like this before in my life.

Calm down! I ordered my racing heart. *What are you doing? Look at those people getting on board. Nothing terrible is happening to them. Relax!*

"May I see your paperwork, ma'am?" The porter asked.

"I don't have any paperwork." My throat felt tight. The next sentence was barely a whisper. "I was told to ask for Sven."

"Your name please?"

"The reservation is for Clayton."

The man turned from me and spoke into a two-way radio.

I tried to breathe in slowly through my nose and release the fear-tainted air through my mouth. What was I frightened of? The ship? That was ridiculous. Even though it was a tremendously gigantic vessel.

"Ms. Clayton?" The porter asked.

"No," I said, hoping my quivering wasn't too obvious. "That's my sister. Joanne Clayton. I'm Holmquist. Melanie. I was a Clayton, but now I'm married." I felt my cheeks flush at my babbling.

"You're not Winifred Clayton?"

"No. She's my aunt. She made the reservation, but she's not here. I'm here."

The porter looked slightly amused. "Sven will come here to meet you. He apologizes for not being on hand when you arrived. Is this your only piece of luggage?"

I nodded and told my mouth to stay shut. This guy didn't want to hear about how I packed every decent stitch I owned, and there was still room for Ethan's Mexican blanket to come home with me.

Stepping to the side, I watched all the non-freaked-out passengers with smiles and eager expressions. One older woman was laughing at something her husband said as he handed the porter a five-dollar bill.

Oh no! I only have Canadian dollars!

That small fact sent my thoughts on a different track. I started planning how I would exchange money when I checked in. Knowing that I had a task to fulfill somehow brought my blood pressure back to normal. Charting out my course of action provided a strange sort of comfort. The panic was gone.

"Ms. Holmquist," a deep voice spoke beside me.

I turned and looked up at Sven, my aunt's personal steward. Every time Aunt Winnie went on a cruise, she was assigned a staff person who would make sure she got settled. Aunt Winnie made it clear to the travel agent that Joanne and I were to receive the same first-class attention to which she was accustomed.

Sven handed me an envelope and let me know with his engaging accent that he would see to my luggage and walk me through the registration process.

"Do you know if my sister has arrived yet?" I asked.

"Yes. She is relaxing at the poolside bar."

I frowned.

Hanging out at a bar? Not my sister. Either he has the wrong sister in mind or Joanne had taken a turn in her life since I last saw her.

"This card needs to be with you at all times," Sven told me after I was given my room key. It looked like a plastic credit card. "You will use it to charge expenditures to your room. Also the time and specified dining room for your dinner reservations is printed on the card."

We passed through another checkpoint, where I slid my plastic card into a machine, looked straight ahead, and had my photo taken.

"I think I blinked," I protested.

"Doesn't matter," the woman in the cruise uniform said.

"It's for identification after you disembark in Ensenada. General features are good enough."

She sounded like a recording. I wondered how many thousands of digital photos of passengers she'd taken during her career and how many had protested like me.

"This way, please." Sven motioned that I should follow him across a secured walkway that led into the ship.

With one foot in front of the other, I held my breath and boarded the ship that had seemed so ominous from a distance. Four short steps led me into what looked like the spacious lobby of a luxury hotel. Two dramatic curved staircases reached to the upper level.

In the center, between the polished stairways, a pianist in a tuxedo was seated at a shiny black grand piano. His rendition of "Swan Lake" filled the glistening lobby with a touch of elegance.

Opulent bouquets of fresh flowers laced the air with sweet fragrance. Dozens of passengers strolled about leisurely in the airy reception area. Many of them held fluted glasses with blended tropical beverages. A waiter meandered from guest to guest, offering appetizers on a silver tray. Oh, yeah. I could see why cruisin' was Aunt Winnie's cup of tea.

I can do this. Why was I so panicked? Did I watch Titanic *one too many times? My problem is that I don't get out enough. I don't know how to act classy in situations like this. But who cares? Joanne and I are going to have the time of our lives!*

⊰⊱

Sisterchicks Do the Hula
Available now!

In five days my best friend, Laurie, and I were scheduled to meet up in Honolulu. What triggered my meltdown was an ordinary box that arrived on my doorstep in the snow. Inside was my maternity bathing suit.

Blithely carrying the box upstairs, I drew the curtains, closed the bedroom door, and peeled off layers of warm clothes. Relieved that the back-ordered item had arrived in time, I wiggled my way into the new swimsuit, slowly turned toward the mirror on the back of the bedroom door, and took in the sight of my blessed belly wrapped in swaddling aqua blue spandex.

First the front view. Then the side. Other side. Twisting my head over my shoulder, I got a glimpse of the backside. Then quickly returned to the front view.

I was shocked! Completely shocked!

The woman in the mirror shook her head at me. *"You're not considering going out in public wearing that, are you?"*

"Yes?" I answered with a woeful sigh. "Although, I didn't think it would look like this on me."

"Oh, really? And just what did you think it would look like on you?"

"Well, not like this."

For months I had been riding high on the "blessed-art-thou-among-women" cloud. I considered it a privilege to carry this baby. I told myself I was participating in a calling that was higher than fashion and charm. Who cares about beauty? The truth was, my body was nurturing new life.

However, truth and beauty had crashed head-on in my bedroom mirror.

"I like this shade of blue," I declared, trying to be positive.

"Yeah? Well, from where I'm standing, that shade of blue does not appear to be too fond of you, sweetheart."

"Maybe I could return this one and order the black one instead."

"Right, because everyone knows that black is always so much more slimming."

"There was that black one with the little pleated skirt..."

"Okay, yeah, there you go. Because nothing says dainty like Shamu in a tutu."

"Hey!" I turned away and covered my belly as if to protect Emilee's ears from this audacious woman. "You don't have to be rude about it!"

"Look who's talking."

I glared over my shoulder at the mannerless minx and found I couldn't say anything. I could only stare at her. At myself. At what I had become. How did this happen?

How could it be that my two dreams had intersected this way? Innocent little Emilee Rose was my dream baby come true. A trip to Hawaii with Laurie was a dream that had waited patiently for two decades to come true.

But someone had taken my two best dreams and poured them into a single test tube when I wasn't looking. Now the churning, foaming result bubbled over the top and ended up larger than life in my bedroom mirror. There she stood, defying me to accept the truth.

I was old.

And I was not beautiful. How had those two facts escaped me in the bliss of being a middle-aged life bearer?

Fumbling my way out of the aqua swimsuit and trying to

stop the ridiculous flow of big, globby tears, I turned my back on the mirror and plunged into my roomiest maternity clothes. Leaning against the ruffled pillows that lined our bedroom window seat, I inched back the curtains and let the tears gush.

Outside, an icy January snowstorm was elbowing its way down the eastern seaboard, causing the limbs of our naked elm tree to shiver uncontrollably. Beside me was a tour book of Hawaii. The cover showed shimmering white sand, pristine blue water, and a graceful palm tree stretching toward the ocean as if offering its hand for the waves to kiss. Beautiful people from all over the world came to bask in the sun and stroll along such exotic beaches in this island paradise.

I glanced sympathetically at the quivering elm tree out my window and tried to imagine slender tropical palms in full sunlight, swaying in the breeze, green and full of life.

"That's right. Think about the beautiful beaches, the sunshine, and all the fun you and Laurie are going to have."

I blew my nose and glanced at the mirror.

She was still there, delivering her sugary sass.

"Don't think of the other tourists—those twenty-year-old toothpicks in their bikinis, sauntering down the beach with their long, cellulite-free legs and their flat stomachs. Who cares that you'll be the only woman on the beach looking like a bright blue Easter egg on parade?"

I picked up a pillow, took aim, and…

The bedroom door swung open, forcing the mirror maven into hiding. My hero entered with a tube of caulking in his hand. "There you are. You okay?"

I clutched the pillow to my middle and nodded.

Darren glanced out the window and then down at the tour book beside me. "I heard this storm is supposed to blow over by Monday. Should be clear sailing when you fly out on Wednesday morning."

"That's what I heard, too." My voice sounded surprisingly steady.

Darren stepped into our bathroom and proceeded to caulk the shower.

"Hope, can you come here and tell me if this looks straight to you?"

I didn't need to go in there to see if his caulking line was straight. Darren's repairs were never straight. But they always worked. That's all that mattered to me.

"Looks good." I tilted my head ever so slightly so that the line along the base of the shower honestly did appear straight.

He glanced up from his kneeling position. With a tender pat on my belly, he said, "And you look good to me."

"Bahwaaaaah!" I burst into tears all over again.

"What's wrong? What did I say?" Darren was on his feet, trying to wrap both arms around me and draw me close. "Why are you crying?"

"How can I possibly look good to you? I'm pregnant! I'm really, really pregnant!"

"Of course you are. Why are you crying?"

"Because I'm going to Hawaii!"

"Yes, you're going to Hawaii. Come on now, pull yourself together."

I kept crying.

Darren looked frantic. He stepped back and, fumbling for his roguish smirk, said, "So, is this a hormone thing?"

"No, it's not a hormone thing! I'm old, Darren! I'm old and pregnant, and I'm going to Hawaii. Can you understand how that makes me feel?"

He couldn't.

How could I possibly expect my husband to understand all the bizarre things that happen to a woman in spirit and flesh when a friendly alien takes over her body? He still couldn't figure out why Laurie and I wanted to fly all the way to Hawaii just to spend a week lounging around a pool, comparing underarm flab, when we could stay home and have the same conversation over the phone for a lot less money.

I took a deep breath. "You know what? I don't care what anyone says. These screaming purple stretch marks running up my biscuit-dough thighs are stripes of honor."

"Exactly."

"I earned every one of those zingers!"

"Of course you did, honey."

"I am a Mother, with a capital M."

"Never doubted it for a moment."

"And everyone knows that aqua is the perfect motherhood color, even in the tropics."

"Especially in the tropics."

"Thank you."

"You're welcome."

What my husband had just observed was a 95 percent hormone-induced solar flare. But there was no way on this blue earth that I would reveal that scientific secret to him.

I concluded my little skit by clearing my throat and saying, "I think your caulking looks good. Very nice."

"Thanks. And I meant what I said. You look good to me, too."

"Thank you." I turned with my chin raised in valor and tried to glide gracefully out of the bathroom, my beach-ball belly exiting a full half a second before the rest of me.

Reaching for the much-debated swimsuit, I rolled it up and tucked it into the corner of my suitcase. Over my shoulder I could feel the mirror maven working up a good sass-and-slash comment. Before she had a chance to deliver it, I turned to face her full on. "Let's see now. One of us is stuck to a piece of particleboard, and one of us is leaving for Hawaii on Wednesday. Any guesses as to which one you are?"

She didn't say a word. She knew her place. And I was about to find mine.

ENJOY ANOTHER DELIGHTFUL ROMANCE SERIES WITH GAYLE ROPER'S SEASIDE SEASONS!

SPRING RAIN
Seaside Seasons Book 1
Leigh Spenser is thrown into conflict when her son's estranged father comes home to Seaside, New Jersey, to comfort his brother dying of AIDS, forcing them to face powerful emotions neither wants to acknowledge. But it's not until their son is kidnapped that Leigh and Clay discover the answers they've been looking for all their lives.

ISBN 1-57673-638-5

SUMMER SHADOWS
Seaside Seasons Book 2
Abby Patterson witnesses a hit-and-run accident but has amnesia and can't remember it. She determines to discover what really happened, endangering herself and her landlord, Marsh Winslow. Marsh, a writer of Westerns, fights the phantoms of his past even as Abby fights chronic pain and struggles with how to honor her overbearing parents.

ISBN 1-57673-969-4

AUTUMN DREAMS

Seaside Seasons Book 3

Cassandra Merton has her hands full with aging parents, a teenage niece and nephew, and a rich bachelor who arrives at her bed-and-breakfast to contemplate his future. When a troubled employee unknowingly endangers Cass, who is taken hostage by a gunman, Dan Harmon realizes his love for Cass.

ISBN 1-59052-127-7

WINTER WINDS

Seaside Seasons Book 4

Pastor Paul Trevelyan hasn't seen the woman he loves in six years. When he's given a second chance with her, he longs to make it work this time. The trouble is, if he doesn't win her back, it could cost him his job—and his happiness. Church discord and a sinister luggage mix-up force the stubborn spouses to take a new look at each other...

ISBN 1-59052-279-6